Johann Friedrich Herbart, Emmie Felkin

An Introduction to Herbart's Science and Practice of Education

Johann Friedrich Herbart, Emmie Felkin

An Introduction to Herbart's Science and Practice of Education

ISBN/EAN: 9783337105242

Printed in Europe, USA, Canada, Australia, Japan

Cover: Foto ©Suzi / pixelio.de

More available books at **www.hansebooks.com**

AN INTRODUCTION

TO

HERBART'S SCIENCE AND PRACTICE OF EDUCATION

BY

HENRY M. AND EMMIE FELKIN

WITH A PREFACE BY
OSCAR BROWNING, M.A.
Fellow of King's College, Cambridge

BOSTON, U.S.A.
PUBLISHED BY D. C. HEATH & CO.
1895

PREFACE

In 1892 Mr. and Mrs. Felkin published a translation of Herbart's *Science of Education* and *The Æsthetic Revelation of the World*, to which I contributed a preface. The book has been well received, and adopted as a text book by the University of Cambridge and other educational bodies. The same writers now increase the debt which is due to them from all advocates of scientific educational training by publishing the present *Introduction to Herbart's Science and Practice of Education*. The object of the book is to answer a question which many students of education are now asking: Who is Herbart? and what did he and his followers teach? It answers this question better than any other account of the Herbartian method hitherto published in English. It is difficult to exhibit adequately the educational views of Herbart by merely translating his works. Herbart's use of philosophical phraseology is peculiar, and it is scarcely possible for any one to comprehend the full meaning of his pedagogical precepts who has not grasped the scope of his philosophy as a whole, an enterprise for which few students of education have either time or opportunity. Besides this, the doctrines of Herbart, like those of Pestalozzi and Froebel, have been developed by a school of Herbartians to conclusions of which, perhaps, Herbart would have approved, but which are not easily discoverable in the text of his writings. The Herbartian doctrine is not simply Herbart; it has been converted into a body of practice. So, while Mr. and Mrs. Felkin have devoted the first chapter of their work to an account of Herbart's psychology and the second to an account of his ethics, they add to their admirable presentation of Herbart's own views on practical teaching a description of the methods of modern German teachers who call themselves "Herbartians."

The book does not attempt more than this. It is an excellent descriptive account of one of the most important pedagogic schools which sprang out of the school of Pestalozzi. If some parts of this account are more satisfactory than others, it is not the fault of the authors. Herbart's own treatment of the questions of government and discipline is not very satisfactory, nor are the difficulties inherent in them cleared up by his successors. If Mr. and Mrs. Felkin fail in this department to carry conviction to English readers, it is because those who preceded them have failed also.

As it is no part of the province of this book to criticise the doctrines of which it gives an account, such a criticism cannot be expected from the writer of the Preface. He would, however, venture to say, as a practical schoolmaster of some experience, that the part of the Herbartian doctrine which carries least conviction to his mind is that of the concentration centres and the historical culture epochs. Any uniformity in *curricula* is, so far as it goes, a hindrance to good education. The faculties of the mind do not develop in the same order in different individuals. The mind in the child and in the young man is always growing, and at a certain normal age it may be considered to be mature; but some minds have developed quickly, others tardily; and, besides this general difference, the tastes for different pursuits at different ages are strongly marked. *Curricula* naturally take but little note of this divergence. They assume the existence of a normal growth, the same for all. Just in proportion as the *curriculum* to which the learner is subject is rigid and uniform, so would it fail to be applicable to a large number of students. An ideal education would be different for every child, because the growths of no two minds are the same. Circumstances may force us to compromise, but we should take care that our compromise gains as much for us and loses as little as possible.

In conclusion I may express my conviction that the present book will prove a most welcome addition to the comparatively small number of works on the scientific study of education which exist in the English language.

OSCAR BROWNING,
*Director of the Cambridge University Day Training College
and Secretary to the Teachers' Training Syndicate.*

KING'S COLLEGE, CAMBRIDGE,
May, 1895.

AUTHORS' PREFATORY NOTE

To Mr. Oscar Browning we and our readers are a second time indebted for a preface to a work on Herbart, and we gladly take this opportunity of cordially thanking him. Our sincere acknowledgments are also due to Prof. James Sully for his kindness in revising the passages on Herbart's use of the term "soul"; to Miss K. M. Clarke for revision of part of the manuscript and for many valuable suggestions; to Dr. Hermann Fehse, of the Real-Gymnasium, Chemnitz, for his careful revision of some of the proofs; and to Herr Geheimerath Müller, the reviser of Hartenstein's edition of Herbart's works for the German press, for ready help and interest in the work.

CHEMNITZ, SAXONY,
April 17th, 1895.

CONTENTS

	PAGE
Preface by Mr. Oscar Browning.	v
Authors' Prefatory Note	vii

INTRODUCTION.

Aim of the work and reasons for undertaking it	1
Spread of Herbartian literature and principles of education	2
Difficulties in the adoption of his system by the elementary and secondary schools of Germany	4
Herbart the first to base education directly on ethics and psychology	7
The three main divisions of the subject	7

(1) Pedagogy, or the science and art of education.
(2) Ethics: its aim.
(3) Psychology: its means.

CHAPTER I.—PSYCHOLOGY.

Education: its possibility, need, importance, justification, motive, work, and aim	11
Herbart's use of the term "soul"	13
The human entity and its endowments, analyzed as an object of education	15
Factors conditioning the teacher's power	17
The senses, the medium for education	17
The three activities of the soul: presentation; feeling; willing	19
Presentations: their origin, classification, laws, varieties, movements, reproduction, and interaction	19
Memory of three kinds: rational, ingenious, and mechanical	30
Suppressed presentations; abstract presentations	32
Psychical and logical concepts	33
Importance of forming an interconnected circle of thought	34
The process of apperception defined	36
Involuntary apperceptive attention	38
Voluntary apperceptive attention	39
Feelings and desires analyzed and classified as secondary states of the soul	40
Herbart's distinction between sensations and feelings	43
Formal feelings; expectation	45
Qualitative feelings; sympathy	47
Desire defined	48
„ dependent on the presentations	51
„ leading to will	51
„ differentiated from feeling	51
„ distinction between, and will	52
„ passing into will	52

CHAPTER II.—ETHICS.

	PAGE
Herbart's definition of ethics	54
The good will	55
The formation of will by insight, the work of education	56
The circle of thought as the source of will	57
Motives, the two classes of, which influence the will	58
Intuitive judgments	59
Ethical judgments developed by the relationships of the will	61
The five practical (moral) ideas	62
Two wills in one person, objective and subjective	62
The first moral idea: inner freedom	63
„ second „ perfection	65
„ third „ benevolence	66
„ fourth „ right	70
„ fifth „ equity	72
The five ideas classified as formal or material	73
„ „ „ combined supply the concept morality	73
The five derived (sociological) ideas	74
Ethics in relation to religion	75
Religion needful to morality	75
„ Herbart's conception of	76
„ in its relation to the child	78

CHAPTER III.—PRACTICAL PEDAGOGY.

SECTION 1.—*Theory of Instruction.*

Formation of character the aim of education	80
Instruction and discipline as means of education	81
Educative instruction	81
Experience and intercourse as teaching the child before attending school	82
The child's store of thought to be examined	82
The child's store of experience and intercourse arranged and extended	83
Presentative instruction depends on apperception	84
Experience and intercourse to be used throughout instruction	84
Instruction, the two lines of	85
analytic; synthetic	85, 86
„ example of, based on experience	86
„ „ intercourse	88
The child's mind must be analyzed to itself	88
Instruction must supplement experience and intercourse	89
Significance of educative instruction	89
Nature of many-sided interest	90
Interest, receptive and apperceptive, compared	91
„ apperceptive, as influencing formation of character	93
„ Herbart's definition of	94
„ far-reaching	94
„ immediate	94
„ many-sided	95

		PAGE
Many-sided interest arising from knowledge is—		
(1) Empirical, with illustrations		96
(2) Speculative ,,		96
(3) Æsthetic ,,		96
Many-sided interest arising from sympathy is—		
(1) Sympathetic		97
(2) Social		97
(3) Religious		97
Interest, illustrations to, arising from sympathy		97
,, an illustration to the six classes of		98
,, balanced		100
,, the motive power in education		101
,, how created		102

Section 2.—*Treatment of the Material of Instruction.*

Classification of the material of instruction 105
Theory of the formal steps 105
Method units 106
,, the aim of 106
The five steps according to Herbart and Rein 107
First formal step: preparation 108
Second ,, presentation 111
Third ,, association 113
Fourth ,, recapitulation 115
Fifth ,, application 116
Principle of the formal steps not new 118
Example of a lesson according to the five formal steps . . 118

Section 3.—*Selection of the Material of Instruction; Dual Theory of the Concentration Centres and Historical Culture Epochs.*

Material, the selection of, discussed 121
,, principle of its selection, as formulated by Ziller . . 122
The eight historical culture epochs 123
Instruction, humanistic and scientific, must be connected . . 123
Humanistic material to be made the concentration centres . . 124
Concentration material, principles for the selection of . . 124
,, ,, epic fairy tales for the first year . . 125
,, ,, *Robinson Crusoe* for the second year . 126
,, ,, for the third and successive years . . 127
Parallel material from German history attached to the centres . 128
The dual theory, general remarks on 129
,, ,, a curriculum based on 130
,, ,, difficulties in the practical working out of . 130
Religious material as concentration centres discussed in the light of Herbart's ethical aim 132

Section 4.

Voigt's criticism on the dual theory as applied to instruction in elementary schools 136

Section 5.

Examples of lessons based on the dual theory of the concentration centres and historical culture epochs 145

CHAPTER IV.—MORAL STRENGTH OF CHARACTER; GOVERNMENT AND DISCIPLINE.

SECTION 1.—*Government.*

	PAGE
Insight alone insufficient to form the will	155
Discipline used for the direct formation of character	156
Government, the aim of	156
„ measures employed by—	
(1) Occupation	157
(2) Supervision	157
(3) Threatening	158
(4) Punishment	158
Reasoning with little children	159
Herbart's view of corporal punishments	160
Authority and love to guide the measures of government	161

SECTION 2.—*Discipline.*

	PAGE
Discipline, the aim of	162
„ and government, contrast between	162
„ must help to form a moral will	163
The principle of apperception applied to formation of will	163
Action of disparate presentations in the formation of will	165
Memory of the will: its conditions	166
Will apperception: its conditions and results	167
"Maxims," Herbart's use of the term	167
The subjective part of character the growth of later years	168
The objective „ „ „ earlier „	168
Desires and their regulation by discipline	169
The personality of the teacher	172
Approbation and blame	172
The joint work of instruction and discipline on character	173
Discipline, relation of, to interest	174
„ measures of	174

CHAPTER V.—THE RELATIONSHIP AND DEBT OF HERBART TO PESTALOZZI 176

CHAPTER VI.—CONCLUSION: SOME ASPECTS OF HERBART'S WORK AND CHARACTER 184

AN INTRODUCTION TO HERBART'S
SCIENCE AND PRACTICE OF EDUCATION

"Die erste und wichtigste aller Fragen, welche der Mensch für sich, für Andere, für den Staat, für die Erziehung, für die Welt, ja sogar in Bezug auf Vorsehung und Erlösung aufwerfen kann, ist die Frage nach der Möglichkeit des Besserwerdens."

—HERBART.

INTRODUCTION

IN 1892, with a view to making Herbart's principles better known in England and America, we published a translation into English of his *Allgemeine Pädagogik*, or *Science of Education*,[1] and with it his short treatise on the *Æsthetic Revelation of the World*. From private communications and many reviews of this translation we gather that although it has been received with much interest and found many careful readers, some difficulty has been experienced by even thoughtful educationists in understanding various parts of Herbart's system, and at times in getting at his real meaning. This is not surprising. Even to German educationists Herbart is a difficult writer, requiring patience and study. The difficulty to an English reader arises from the fact that the whole tone of thought is new and strange, the terminology is unknown to him, and the knowledge assumed which forms the basis upon which the science is built up, is mostly wanting, or wanting in the form and connection required by Herbart. Ufer, an educationist himself and one of Herbart's best popular expositors, whose work *Vorschule der Pädagogik Herbart's* we shall make free use of in the following pages, refers in his introduction to this initial difficulty in the study of Herbart. "The reader," he says, "can easily imagine how I plagued myself uselessly when he remembers Herbart's peculiar use of language, and further considers that there are many parts of Herbart's pedagogy which cannot be understood by those who are not acquainted with the auxiliary sciences in Herbartian form which underlie it." It was this same difficulty which

---

[1] Boston: D. C. Heath & Co.

led him to write his valuable little work for those beginning the study of Herbart.

In our introduction to the translation above mentioned, we gave a slight sketch of Herbart's uneventful life and important educational work, and attempted to supply the reader with some of this necessary preliminary knowledge as an aid to understanding the translation. But the space at our disposal was insufficient to give that fuller knowledge, especially of Herbart's psychology, which the reader requires to enter with interest and profit upon a study of his educational system. Our object, then, in the following pages, is to supply this preliminary need, to give the preparatory data sufficient to make the *Science of Education* comprehensible to a thoughtful reader or an intelligent teacher seeking help in his daily work. We shall not attempt to explain individually, or in the order in which they occur, the obscure passages and terms left undefined by Herbart; our object will rather be to enable the student, after reading this preparatory sketch, to do so for himself. To this end we shall try to give an outline of Herbart's psychology, ethics, and pedagogy, supplying practical illustrations where such aid is necessary to render his meaning clearer.

A friend once remarked that he never understood a sermon of Dr. Martineau's till he had heard the last word. The reader will have to exercise similar patience with Herbart, and often wait for the last word to illuminate the whole chapter.

The materials have been partly gathered from the two works Herbart wrote as supplementary to the *Pädagogik*, the one *Umriss pädagogischer Vorlesungen*, published in 1835, the other *Umriss der Allgemeinen Pädagogik*, which appeared four years later. For a few of the practical illustrations, for the general idea of the book, and for some of its material we are indebted to Ufer's work above mentioned.[1]

It is now more than half a century since Herbart's death, and the seed he spent his life in sowing is bearing fruit. His influence in Germany has rapidly extended during the last

---

[1] Charles Ufer, formerly teacher at Elberfeld and since 1886 teacher in the Higher Girls' School at Altenburg, in Saxony, where the instruction given is based on Herbart's theory.

thirty years, and has spread into other countries. In Germany societies have been formed for promoting education on the lines of his educational principles, as well as for discussion and mutual help. The first of these, representing the Rhine districts and Westphalia, comprised over 400 members. Later on meetings were held in East Germany, and then in Bavaria and Wurtemberg, for extending the work of the societies. Afterwards an important society was formed for Thuringia, and lastly another for Saxony. The Thuringian society has its headquarters at Jena, to whose university a school is attached, wherein Herbart's principles, as elaborated by Ziller and the modern school, are practically applied. Prof. Rein, Lecturer on Pedagogy at the university, is president of this society and the acknowledged present leader of the modern Herbartian movement. The formation of this society for Middle Germany, with many affiliated sub-societies, which send delegates to the annual meeting, is a new proof of the rapidly increasing influence of Herbart's principles. It holds its annual conference at Erfurt, and the first meeting in 1892 was attended by over 2,000 educationists, when Prof. Rein was elected president of the council for three years. It has been stated by a competent authority that more than half the teachers in Germany, especially those in the secondary schools, such as the Gymnasien, Real, higher mercantile, etc., are disciples of Herbart.

In Austria, Hungary, the Balkan States, Armenia, his followers are to be found, and attempts are being made to introduce his works into Italy and France by means of translations. Ufer mentions especially Edouard Roehrich's *Théorie de l'Education d'après les Principes de Herbart* [1] as a good work. In Holland De Raaf has translated Dörpfeld's book *Über Denken und Gedächtniss*, besides writing a popular introduction to Herbart's *Psychology*. In the United States, where Prof. de Garmo is his most enthusiastic advocate, he is widely known. Prof. de Garmo has founded a Herbart society in Saratoga, besides having translated several works of the Herbartian school, such as Lange *On Apperception*, and pub-

---

[1] Paris, 1884: Delegrave.

lished various treatises and articles. The educational press in the States has been favourable to the Herbartian movement, and some of the reviews closely follow its development in Germany. This work has steadily progressed owing to the continued efforts of the Herbartian school, represented by such men as Ziller (now dead), Dörpfeld, Rein, Lange, Drübal, Lindner, Wolkmann, Ballauf, Kern, Willman, Pickel, Scheller, and others, whose works, elucidating, developing, and practically applying Herbart's ideas, are studied by a large number of German teachers. Their efforts have been mainly devoted on the one hand, to working out into a complete system Herbart's science of education on its theoretical side, and on the other to developing it into a practical method or art. Herbart originally applied his system to secondary education only; his followers' strenuous work has been to remould all education, elementary and secondary, according to that system. In doing this they have undoubtedly gone beyond Herbart in some of their developments, and it would be an interesting study to trace out, by comparison with Herbart's original principles, how far they have remained true to them. We shall attempt to do this later on in regard to the dual theory of the historical culture grades and concentration centres. The great initial difficulty lay in the want of suitable manuals, but this has been partly overcome by the publication of a number of practical works, especially during the last sixteen years, handbooks for teaching, chiefly in elementary schools, various subjects on strictly Herbartian principles.[1]

Ufer attributes much of the rapid spread of Herbart's influence to the publication of these practical works. Although, as we have seen, Herbart's principles have exerted a powerful influence on German education, it must not be supposed that his system as such, has been adopted to any great extent in

---

[1] Eberhardt: *Poetry in the Elementary Schools* (Langensalza: Beyer); Staude: *Preparations for Histories of the Old and New Testaments* (Dresden: Bleyl); Thrändorf: *Religious Instruction in the Higher Classes of Elementary Schools* (Dresden: Bleyl); Staude and Göppert: *Preparations for German History* (Dresden: Bleyl); Fritzsche: *German History in the People's Schools (Modern)* (Altenburg: Pierer); Matzat: *Method of Geographical Instruction* (Berlin: Parey).

either the secondary or elementary schools in Germany. These being for the most part communal, municipal, and state schools, a considerable unanimity of opinion is required before changes can be made in their curricula and methods of teaching. Though Herbart's wide spread influence on teachers must necessarily permeate the schools, and some of his principles are carried out in certain branches of instruction, his system has by no means found such unanimous acceptance as to make more direct and radical changes possible. Perhaps one chief reason for this is, that all elementary schools in Germany, except the purely technical ones, are denominational—either Lutheran or Catholic—and the position which religious instruction occupies in Herbart's system can only with difficulty be accommodated to such conditions. The building up of a firmly established self-contained moral character through the operation of the *enlightened* will was, as the reader will perceive for himself, the goal of all Herbart's educational efforts. From the beginning of his career to its close, this was kept clearly in view, and it determined the whole course of his educational thought, work, and investigations. Knowledge, while always subordinate to this main aim, and indeed only valuable in so far as it furthers it, was an indispensable condition to its attainment, for with Herbart ignorance and morality could not exist together. "Stupid people," he says, "cannot be virtuous" (*Stumpfsinnige können nicht tugendhaft sein*[1]). The school then was to do its part by training the disposition and storing the mind with knowledge. It was to supply its share of the material which *must* be present for the will to act upon, and in the active manipulation of which that will, with such aid as the teacher could give, must gradually work out its own enlightenment. This work in the school was to be carried on in a religious atmosphere and warmed by religious feeling. But the *direct* teaching of religion as such, at least in early years, was to be left to the Church, and still more to the home. Even there, to judge from Herbart's words hereafter quoted,[2] it was principally to take forms other than those of dogmas or

---

[1] *Umriss pädagogischer Vorlesungen*, p. 64.   [2] *Ibid.*, p. 92.

confessions of faith, forms compatible with his theory of morality—a theory based on the mind's intuitive judgments,[1] and not on religion in the common acceptation of that term. The more modern Herbartian school, on the contrary, instead of making the formation of a moral character the great end of education, has set up in its place the formation of a sound Lutheran Christian, and makes formal religious instruction the starting-point from which all other instruction, even of the natural sciences, proceeds. It uses, as we shall hereafter describe, the religious material for the " concentration centres " and " historical culture grades," as the backbone of the whole system of instruction. It is open to grave doubt whether such a use is a true outcome of Herbart's principles, whether it is not rather the result of an effort on the part of his followers to limit the principles which Herbart held to be of universal application by local conditions of thought and faith.

Education being, in Herbart's words, " a vast whole of ceaseless labour, which exacts true proportion from beginning to end," obviously needs a plan or system. To influence the soul[2] aright, a knowledge of its laws is absolutely needful; hence the teacher requires to be acquainted with the science of psychology.

---

[1] Intuitive judgments form the basis of Herbart's system of ethics. They are to him an ultimate fact of consciousness, independent of the will, standing, as it were, opposite to it, and estimating the value of its acts. The essence of these judgments is the perception, present says Herbart, in every human soul, that to it individually, right and wrong are inconvertible terms; and their universal expression is consciousness pronouncing to itself the distinction for it between right and wrong. The *standard* by which the intuitive judgments estimate the will's acts changes with the changing states of human thought; but the *judge* (the intuitive judgment), which, whatever the standard may be, pronounces to the individual whether he and his fellow-creatures attain in their separate acts of will to the standard or fall short of it, is a constant power in every human soul. Since the intuitive judgments are involuntary and absolute, springing up whenever the question of moral worth or worthlessness has to be determined. and are utterly without proof, since none is possible, they are analogous in nature with the judgments which we pass without any logical evidence on musical harmonies and discords on hearing them. On the strength of this analogy, based on the involuntary origin and certainty without proof, between the judgments of will and those of art, Herbart extends the term *æsthetic* judgments to the intuitive judgments as well as to those passed on art proper.

[2] For Herbart's use of the term *soul*, see p. 13.

It is the handmaid of pedagogy. Herbart says of it, "Psychology is the primary auxiliary science of the teacher; we must have it before we can say of a single lesson what has been taught rightly and what wrongly."

But this large and complicated task has an aim, viz., to build up a moral character. The teacher has to lead the child to the knowledge of good and evil, to train his will to choose the good, and to enable him of himself to keep thereto and continue to make it the law of his life. For active perception of this aim in general, as well as in individual parts, a knowledge of ethics or practical philosophy [1] is needful, and it is thus the second assistant science of pedagogy.

Herbart was the first to base pedagogy, the science of education, directly on ethics and psychology, and this is his great work for, and service to mankind. From ethics he derived the end and aim of all teaching: virtue; from psychology, the means whereby it is compassed. He is the founder of modern educational psychology; he made the *implicit* psychology latent in the best of teaching before his time *explicit*. As mathematics are the basis of astronomy, so is psychology the only trustworthy basis for any true science of education, and only by the application of that science to the art of education can any certitude be obtained as to its methods and results. Education has hitherto been, and even now is, one of the most uncertain and unsatisfactory of all arts, for it is one in which the practical worker is least certain of his results. Herbart's ideal was a science of education which, translated into practice, *must* compass its aim. That aim, again—virtue—if the possibility of its universal attainment were to be proved, also needed a firm and universal foundation, and this Herbart found in the intuitive judgments of the mind.[2] In the mind then he sought and found solid rock, the certitude for both his aim and his means.

We have thus three main divisions of our subject: (1)

---

[1] Practical philosophy is the doctrine of what ought to be as distinguished from general philosophy, or the doctrine of what "is." Whenever practical philosophy is mentioned, morality, or the science of it—ethics—is intended. [2] See note, p. 6.

pedagogy, or the science of education ; (2) *ethics*, whence we derive its aim ; (3) *psychology*, whence we derive its means. Herbart, as a practical teacher, began with pedagogy; this led him to study psychology, and later on ethics in relation to formation of character. Then all three combined, and developed in his mind for the remainder of his life, each forming and being formed by the others. His psychological and ethical studies were always carried on and utilized with a view to the work he had set himself to accomplish, viz., the establishment of education on a scientific foundation. The results of his experience and labours were given to the public from time to time in many volumes, of which the *Science of Education* was one of the earlier, and was written before his *Psychology*. This inversion of scientific sequence is one of the main causes of the difficulty many readers have found in understanding the *Science of Education*.

The student therefore who begins the study of it expecting to find it a compact and complete science of psychology will be disappointed. Scattered throughout the book are numerous pregnant psychological statements, and, it must be confessed, side by side with them many dark sayings, the terminology of which alone must leave the reader who is ignorant of Herbart's later psychological works in doubt as to their meaning. The cause of this has already been indicated. The *Science of Education* was the outcome of Herbart's practical work as a teacher, while the greater part of its theoretical groundwork lay in his mind unformulated at the time it was written. The formulation of the pyschological basis of the theory of education was, as he says in the introduction to the *Science of Education*, at that time only "a pious wish." It is true that he began his study of psychology during his teacher years in Berne with an attempt to calculate and express the working of elementary psychologic laws in terms of mathematics. But Herbart's own words, as well as the internal evidence of the *Science of Education*, prove that no system of psychology was formulated by him till long after its appearance in 1806. In a letter of 1831 to his friend Schmidt on "The Application of Psychology to Education," he writes, "The *Science of Education* is incomplete, for although, as the title says, it is deduced from the aim of education, the psychology, which I was at that time only beginning to search for, is deficient." Again, in his announcement of the *Outlines of Educational Lectures* in 1835 he writes, " The psychology of the author was worked out and written down during many years of educational activity, and rose in great part out of the experiences acquired thereby."

Something of the same difficulty, though arising from a different cause, will be felt by the reader in understanding the ethical element in the *Science of Education*. Many of the terms found there—for instance, the idea of benevolence, the idea of perfection, the objective and subjective sides of character—are used by Herbart in a sense peculiarly his own, and they therefore only receive their explanation and significance when the connotation he gives them is fully understood.

But notwithstanding the obscurity of the psychology and ethics found in the *Science of Education*, there is a vital bond, as the student will discover for himself, between them and Herbart's scheme of education. "Through the teacher's aim, education is connected with practical philosophy; in the consideration of ways and means and obstacles thereto, it is connected with psychology."[1] Therefore the understanding of those sciences so far as they form the basis of his *Science of Education* is obviously indispensable to its comprehension and use.

The reader, who, it is presumed, is still unfamiliar with the translation before referred to of the *Allgemeine Pädagogik (Science of Education)* and the Introduction thereto contained in the same volume, will, it is suggested, find it advantageous at this point to turn to the general summary of Herbart's philosophy and principles of education given therein from pp. 24 to 56. By reading it, he will obtain a general outline of the whole subject, the details of which are to be filled in by degrees through later study. This summary could have been introduced at this point, but as it can be found there, and space is limited, it is unnecessary to repeat it here. In all that follows

[1] *Briefe Herbart's.*

therefore it is presumed that the reader has made himself acquainted with it. He is therefore recommended to take his course of Herbart as follows:—

1. The sketch of Herbart's life and educational work and also the summary of his philosophy and principles of education contained between pp. 1 and 56 in the *Science of Education*, then—
2. The present work as a preparation to—
3. The general principles of the *Science of Education* from p. 78 to the end, and—
4. The æsthetic revelation of the world as found from pp. 57 to 77, containing Herbart's ideal aim for education.

In the succeeding pages, we shall, while following the three main divisions of the subject before named, attempt to give first a sketch of Herbart's educational pyschology, then an outline of his ethical theory and aim, and lastly of his practical pedagogy, as the application of his psychology to the art of teaching. Connected with this some references to developments of the modern Herbartian school will be necessary; they are interesting especially in regard to the dual theory of the concentration centres and the historical culture grades, which has latterly given rise to much warm debate in educational circles in Germany.

CHAPTER I

PSYCHOLOGY

The possibility of education. The possibility of education rests for Herbart a first principle of his psychology, *i.e.*, the capacity of the human will for cultivation.[1] This capacity is revealed during the process of cultivation by the transition of the will from a state of impetuosity and capriciousness to a state of stability. The power of education is, however, not unlimited. It is conditioned by the individuality and environment of the child.

The need for education. The necessity for education Herbart finds in his conviction, that the child's mind is in its very nature undetermined either for good or ill when it comes into the world. The mind, unlike the body of the child and the varied forms of the animal and vegetable world, does *not* move during its life on earth to an end predetermined in the germ. For it is built up entirely of presentations[2] which, received

---

[1] *Umriss pädagogischer Vorlesungen.*

[2] By a presentation Herbart means not only the combination of various sensations by the mind, which we call a percept, but the single sense impressions of which a percept is composed. These impressions supply the mind with its primordial presentations—those of sight, touch, taste, etc.—from which all the after-contents of the mind are derived. The primordial presentations constitute, however, but a small part of the mind's contents; their interaction produces the derived presentations, which in their varied developments form the greater part thereof. Presentations once created, the recurrence of the sensuous impression, which necessarily entered into the process, is unnecessary; they are an abiding portion of the mind's contents, playing their part, now one of *re*-presentation in consciousness, without further aid from the special sense organs. Those among them which are the distinct and absolute reflection of the thing or idea which caused them are capable of development by the processes of comparison, abstraction, generalization, into concepts (indirect sensuous presentations) which form the material for the higher and highest processes of thought. For the union of two concepts in a proposition involves an act of judgment, and the inference or conclusion, the induction or deduction

primarily through the senses, subsequently in their combinations, changes, and interactions, constitute all the manifold forms of consciousness. A plant develops to a predetermined form; an animal must fulfil the work of its nature: its instincts compel it to a consequent activity. From the human being, possessed of intelligence instead of instinct, no such consequent course of action can be inferred. "He, who may become a wild animal or personified reason, who is unceasingly moulded by circumstances—he needs the art which can so build that he may receive the right form."[1] It is folly to expect this, as Rousseau did, from nature, and still greater folly to await it from chance.

The importance of education. The importance of education follows immediately from Herbart's proof of its necessity. If the mind is built up of presentations, and is inherently neither good nor bad, but develops one way or other under external influence and the guidance of the teacher, it follows that what it receives in the form of presentations and their mode of combination—that is to say, the work of education—is of infinite importance.

Education justified. The justification for education Herbart finds in the fact that the child begins life without a will of his own, and so cannot enter into moral relations with himself and the world around him. To the wild impetuosity which he at first possesses, and which is a principle of disorder, impelling him hither and thither, the term *will* cannot be applied.[2]

The motive for education. The natural and noblest motive for education Herbart finds in the love for children.[3]

The work of education. The work of education is to form the circle of thought by means of government, an educating instruction, and discipline; to build up the store of that which passes by degrees from interest to desire, and thence through action to the formation of the will. It is a "vast whole of ceaseless labour, which exacts true proportion from beginning to end."

---

we draw from such judgments involves an act of reasoning (*Science of Education*, p. 33).
[1] *Standpunkt der Beurtheilung der Pestalozischen Methode.*
[2] *Science of Education*, Book I., chap. 1. [3] *Ibid.*, Book I., chap. 2.

The aim of education. Finally, the aim of education is to form such a circle of thought that from it a good will—that is, a will obedient to right insight (*Einsicht*)[1]—may arise.

Herbart's use of the term "soul." Education assumes a soul in the child upon which it can work. Before examining the grounds of the assumption that the child *has* a soul, the meaning Herbart attaches to the term must be explained.

Psychologists like Bain and Sully use "mind" to signify the *sum* of the states of knowing, feeling, and willing, experienced by an individual. They say nothing of an immaterial substance in which the states of knowing, feeling, and willing arise. Ward, for example, views psychical phenomena as related to a formal subject or *ego*; Herbart, on the contrary, views them as related to a metaphysical substance. To this non-material substance, of which he always takes account, he gives the name *soul*. The primary activity of the soul is presentation, and this primary activity he calls *geist*, a term sometimes translated mind, sometimes intellect. Feeling, desire, volition, are states arising from the interaction of the presentations. These states Herbart calls *gemüth*, *i.e.*, the disposition, or, as he himself terms it, "the heart." "So far as it presents or conceives, the soul is called intellect (*geist*); so far as it feels and desires, it is called disposition or heart (*gemüth*). The disposition has its source in the mind; in other words, feeling and desiring are conditions, and for the most part changeable conditions, of the presentations."[2]

Herbart conceived of the soul as a simple, unchanging being, originally without any plurality of states, activities, or powers; on its union with the body it becomes the bearer of the presentations, which, as hereafter explained, mutually conflict with and suppress or fuse with each other in consciousness. Herbart believed the psychical activity of this distinct spiritual

---

[1] Right insight, as Herbart uses the term, is the resultant of two conditions: (1) that the circle of thought shall contain a store of truth—*i.e.*, a correspondence between the order of its ideas and the order of phenomena ; (2) that the individual possessing such a circle of thought shall actively use it in the effort to discern and assimilate (apperceive) new moral and intellectual truth. Right insight thus covers what is ethically *good* and intellectually *true*. [2] *Lehrbuch zur Psychologie*.

substance to be, like the physical energy of the material world, indestructible. On this ground he held the soul to be immortal. "He considered the argument from design to be as valid for Divine activity as for human, and to justify the belief in a supersensible reality, concerning which, however, exact knowledge is neither attainable nor on practical grounds desirable."[1]

The meaning attached by Herbart to "soul" precludes the substitution of any other term for it here.[2] But the student is reminded that, as the basis of his psychology, it includes as its modes of manifestation, like the term *mind* before referred to when used by psychologists, knowing, feeling, and willing. It is permissible to use the terms *mind* and *soul* as interchangeable so long as the classification of their manifestations is under consideration. A step farther back, however, when the relation of these manifestations to each other is the subject of inquiry, the radical distinction between the terms comes forth, and will become clear to the student when he has mastered Herbart's theories of feeling, desire, and will.

The independent existence of the soul indicated. What is our ground for assuming the child has a soul? What are our reasons for rejecting the materialistic assertion that everything which we call spiritual is but a state of the corporeal?

Look at a piece of sugar. The rays of light emerging from it penetrate successively the several parts of the eye until they strike the retina. The process, to this point physical (optical), now becomes physiological. The extremities of the optic nerve situated in the retina take up the stimulus transferring it to the optic nerve itself and thence to the brain. The vibration of a certain brain fibre is, according to materialism, synonymous with the consciousness of the stimulus.

If I place the sugar on my tongue, and afterwards take it in my hand, other sets of nerves—*i.e.*, those of taste and touch —successively carry the stimulus by the same process to the brain, setting in vibration in each case, however, a different set of brain fibres.

---

[1] Article on Herbart, *Encyclopædia Britannica*.
[2] This opinion is confirmed by Prof. Sully.

Now, when we think of a piece of sugar, it occurs to us that it is white, *and* sweet, *and* heavy. Hence we see that the impression did not *merely* set certain brain fibres in motion, but that something *beyond* this—*i.e.*, a combination—has taken place. This combination is only conceivable on the assumption of an existence other than the body, an existence Herbart calls soul. Beyond the physical and physiological processes there is the psychological, and materialism, treating the mental only as a function of the material, can in no way explain this *combination* of impressions. We find it in a simple percept when we apprehend an external object by combining various sensations, in sugar, for example, those of sight, taste, and touch; we find it in the re-presentation of the percept when we combine the impressions of the sensations, the sugar being no longer present; and we find it in every higher stage of mental activity. It was this power, the power of memory, which caused Kant to characterize consciousness as a synthesis.

Interconnection of body and soul. But in differentiating soul from body we must not lose sight of a fact of experience of great importance to the teacher, *i.e.*, that each reacts on the other. Modern investigation tends to prove that "for every phenomenon in the world of consciousness there is a corresponding phenomenon in the world of matter, and conversely (so far as there is reason to suppose that conscious life is correlated with material phenomena)." As Prof. Höffding has shown, "the parallels between the activity of consciousness and the functions of the nervous system point to such a relation, and it would be an amazing accident if, while the characteristic marks repeated themselves in this way, there were not at the foundation an inner connection."[1] *What* the nature of the connection is we cannot tell. Its practical expression for the teacher is that the health or disease of each is a cause of the health or disease of the other.

The teacher has to do with the human entity plus its endowments. Turning now to the exclusive consideration of mental phenomena, we see how much more varied and extensive are the contents of an adult's mind than those of a little child's, and the little child's

---
[1] *Outlines of Psychology*, Prof. Höffding, chap. ii., pp. 50-64.

again than those of an infant. We may presume the new-born child has no mind contents of any importance. Herbart's belief, founded partly on metaphysics and partly on his own observations, was that the soul has originally no contents, but begins to acquire them as soon as it enters into union with the body. Since the soul has in itself (in its essence[1]) no contents, the term *endowment* cannot be applied to it as such. The souls of all human beings are alike in substance. When Herbart and his school speak of the soul's lack of endowments, we must remember they refer to a state anterior to its union with the body. Now the teacher has to do solely with the union of body and soul, and he finds, at the stage when he comes in contact with it, certain endowments already present.

Inborn endowments. *Firstly*, it has what we may call inborn endowments—the result of the bodily nature. No two human bodies exist which are identical in all their parts. Given this cause alone, the essential life of every human being must be something peculiar to itself, for the body influences the soul. In other words, the mind, through the medium of the nervous system, enters into reciprocal relations with the external world, and the more perfect that system the richer may be the store of sensuous impressions, and hence of mind contents.[2]

Acquired endowments. *Secondly*, there are acquired endowments arising from the environment which birth assigns to every human being, and which are necessarily peculiar to each. The factors of which this environment is composed are twofold, locality and human society, and each of them has its share of

---

[1] All that exists exists *in se* or *in alio*, either in itself or through something else. Colour, weight, small, exist only in something other than themselves, *i.e.*, in substantials to whose nature they belong. The stuff on which they act exists in itself, in *se*. The latter is called *substance* (reality, essence); the former are called *adherents* (accidents). The relation between substance and accidents, which in popular parlance is expressed by the word *have*, is termed *inherence*. The soul, then, is a substance; its contents are adherents.

[2] Herbart expresses this thus:—" The mind, according to the physical form in which it is embodied, finds in its functions sundry difficulties, and conversely relative facilities " (*Science of Education*, p. 118).

influence on the child. "The inborn is an heirloom; the habits acquired in earliest years are a dowry."[1]

Herbart estimates the great influence of environment in determining the nature of the acquired endowments, and thus in preparing the ground for the teacher, as follows:—" In the case of those who as children are subjected to the guidance of various persons, and shuffled about among different houses and conditions of life, we usually find masses of presentations which are inconsistent with each other, and are badly connected. It is difficult to obtain their perfect confidence, for they nourish secret wishes and feel contrasts which are difficult to discover, and some follow tendencies which education cannot countenance. Far more capable of culture are those who have always been trained for a long time by one person (the mother being the best), and have not been accustomed to conceal their inner life from that person. Then the great thing is to join the further education on to that already existent, and to demand no leaps of thought from the child."[2]

Factors conditioning the teacher's power. We may infer from the preceding that two pupils, taught and treated in precisely the same manner by the teacher, would develop into identical human beings if—

1. Their bodies were absolutely alike.
2. If their acquired endowments were the same.
3. If the hidden and uncontrollable influences which affect education, and are beyond the teacher's knowledge and control, were precisely the same in kind and degree.

These factors, however, never are identical, and even where environment appears to be absolutely the same the children in its midst will develop differently. The power of the teacher is therefore conditioned by the sum of the child's inborn and acquired endowments, in other words, roughly speaking, by his individuality.[3]

The senses are the medium for education. All education, according to Herbart, takes place through the medium of the body. The sense organs are the doors through which entrance to

---

[1] *Letters on the Application of Psychology to Pedagogy*, No. 4.
[2] *Umriss pädagogischer Vorlesungen*, 33.
[3] *Science of Education*, Translator's Introduction, p. 34.

C

the mental life is obtained, and the mind contains nothing which has not initially entered it through them. Hence, the more perfect the senses, the richer *may* be the contents of the mind, though it does not necessarily follow they must be so.

That a human being has good sense organs is not sufficient The objects upon which to exercise them must also be present. "You remember," says Carlyle, "that fancy of Plato's of a man who had grown to maturity in some dark distance, and was brought on a sudden into the upper air to see the sun rise. With the *free, open sight* of a child, yet with the ripe faculty of a man, his whole heart would be kindled by the sight." Again, the boy in Jean Paul's *Levana* appreciates the beauty of the world, when he first sees it after a childhood spent in a subterranean chamber. Both he and Plato's child-man are indeed creatures of the imagination. A child, who had not been allowed to receive a number of sense impressions, would be neither capable of instruction, nor of perceiving the external world aright, much less of appreciating its beauty. Rousseau is truer to fact than either Carlyle or Richter. His Emile has a correct visual impression of the sun because his eye has been accustomed to its light Its rising arouses his curiosity, the legitimate, because natural, feeling at his age; but he cannot appreciate its beauty, "because the complex and momentary impression of all these sensations requires an experience he has never gained."[1] Compare with these instances the recorded experiences of Caspar Hauser. Set free after having spent his youth in a dark room, he was shown the beautiful view from the tower of Nuremberg, and he drew back in fear. When questioned later as to his behaviour, he said, "On looking out of the window it seemed to me as if just before my eyes, there were a shutter on which a painter had splashed a hotch-potch of colours—white, red, yellow, green, blue. Single things, as I now see them, I could not then distinguish. I was obliged to convince myself later during my walks, that what I had seen were fields, mountains, and houses." The senses then need cultivation and exercise. Like

---

[1] Rousseau's *Émile*, Miss Worthington's translation, p. 125.

a lock gate, they must be opened, that the external world may stream into the mind. They must be made sensitive like a photographic plate, that the manifold objects of the external world may be imprinted in pictures, clear, sharp, and enduring, upon the mind. As sight is "the leading avenue" of perception, the term which Pestalozzi used, and which means literally sight perception, may be extended to all perceptions or "observations" made through the other senses. This term is *Anschauung*, the act of observing the qualities of an object and then combining them in the mind.

Presentation, feeling, and willing.
If we examine our mental life, we find that something appears to take place *in* us without any expenditure of power on our part; this is *presentation*. Again, something else appears to take place *with* us, so that we are pleasurably or painfully affected by it; this is *feeling*. And yet again, something else appears to go *out* of us as our own doing, and to this the general term *willing* or *acting* is applied.

In the older systems of psychology, as elsewhere explained,[1] intellect, feeling, and will were considered to be distinct capacities or faculties of the soul. Herbart, on the contrary, considered these three activities to be simply modes of one element common to all. He founded his proof on experience, metaphysics, and mathematics. We can here only explain his theory of mental life in so far as it rests on experience.

Presentation.
First, in regard to *presentation*, he held that we acquire all presentations primarily through the medium of the senses in the following manner. If I handle a piece of sugar, then look at it, and finally place it in my mouth, I receive impressions of heaviness, of whiteness, and of sweetness. These impressions, singly called sensations, are the primordial presentations, and are comprehended in the mind as the "image" or "idea" of sugar. This idea, created from single sense impressions, we call an observation.[2] It is the

---

[1] Introduction to *Science of Education*, p. 32.
[2] The term *Anschauung*, used here by Herbart, is translated in this book, as throughout the *Science of Education*, by the word *observa-*

complex of collective impressions which we have of a thing. "Observations," whether acquired through the different senses, or through one sense, are formed not by a simple, but by a complex, act. Sensations of sight, touch, and taste, are elements in the observation of an orange. An observation of a rose at a distance where only one sense—that of sight—is employed, also involves numerous sense impressions (of red, green, round, etc.). In both cases the mind is active in combining the sense impressions, and it is the sum of them which gives the "observation" of an orange or of a rose.

The origin of perceptions through the senses. Touch and sight each supply us with a number of sense impressions of one object—its form, density, size. Hearing, taste, and smell each give us respectively but one sense impression. Therefore touch and sight are the most important senses in acquiring "observations," because the knowledge we obtain through them of objects is more extended than that given by the other senses.

Each sense is affected by different stimuli—the sight, for instance, by the rays of light which we perceive in various degrees of light and shades of colour. In a white ball, the ray of light emitted by the point in the upper surface nearest to me is the lightest; the more remote parts emit darker rays.

---

tion, but it must be carefully noted, this, though in some respects the best rendering, is by no means an equivalent for *Anschauung.* Mr. Quick writes of attempted renderings thus (*Educational Reformers,* p. 361): "'Sense impression' has lately been tried for *Anschauung*; but this is in two ways defective, for (1) there may be *Anschauungen* beyond the range of the senses, and (2) there is in an *Anschauung* an active as well as a passive element, and this the word 'impression' does not convey. The active part is brought out better by 'observation,' the word used by Joseph Payne and James MacAlister, but this seems hardly wide enough. Other writers of English borrow words straight from the French, and talk about 'intuition' and 'intuitive,' words which were taken (first, I believe, by Kant) from the Latin *intuere,* ' to look at *with attention and reflection.*'" "Intuition," in this its strictly etymological sense, is the term Mr. Quick chooses, but there is a misleading popular use of it, which seems to make avoidance of it, if possible, desirable. The term "observation," here chosen, is a fairly satisfactory equivalent for *Anschauung,* if Mr. Sully's definition of observation as "*regulated perception*" be kept in mind—that is, "perception into which a special degree of mental activity is thrown, so that what is present may be carefully and accurately noted" (*Teacher's Psychology,* Prof. Sully, p. 144).

The importance of the sense of touch now becomes apparent. The rays of light will give me no knowledge of the shape of the body, unless my sense of touch has been previously active about it. Movement of the tactile organ in a gradually changing direction must have given me the idea of roundness. Then I perceive a certain arrangement of light and shade goes with the form, which active touch has proved to me to be spherical. Finally, after these experiences of touch and sight have become associated, and I know that an object of spherical form is accompanied by this particular condition of the rays of light, I conclude on seeing it that the ball in question, at least on the side turned towards me, is rounded. So when I attribute a spherical form to a body in looking at it, I *infer* the form from the nature of the rays of light, but do not perceive it immediately. "We translate visual impressions into terms of the earlier and more elementary experiences of active touch. Seeing is thus to a large extent a representative process and an interpretative act of the mind. First because the knowledge of geometric properties is fuller and more direct in the case of touch than in that of sight, and second because with respect to the important mechanical properties—hardness, weight, etc.—our knowledge is altogether derived from touch, tactile apprehension is to be regarded as the primary and most fundamental form of perception." [1]

In the sense of touch, we must distinguish between touch proper—the consciousness of contact—and general skin sensibility. The most highly sensitive parts of the tactile organ are the tongue, finger-tips, and lips. Democritus, 2,300 years ago, recognized the importance of tactual sense as the basis of all the senses, and its influence upon the development of intelligence is proved by Herbert Spencer. The parrot has the greatest tactual power, and is the most intelligent of birds, for it acquires knowledge impossible to birds which cannot use their feet as hands; the elephant is the most intelligent of quadrupeds, the basis of its sagacity being the number of ex-

---

[1] *Teacher's Psychology* Prof. Sully, pp. 135, 137.

periences it owes to its wonderfully adaptable trunk; the more intelligent apes, again, have increasing tactual range and delicacy. The tactual sense is, as it were, the mother-tongue of all the senses, into which it must be translated to be of service to the organism.[1]

Definition of presentation. That which remains of a sense impression in the soul after the physical stimulus which creates it has ceased, is called by Herbart a presentation (*Vorstellung*).

Herbart distinguishes as an *Empfindung* that which exists of a sense impression in the soul *while* the physical stimulus is still going on (a percept). But since he divides all manifestations of soul into primary activities and secondary states, and *Empfindungen* are primary activities, arising from the union of body and soul, which cannot be analyzed further, they fall under the general term *Vorstellung*. They are the elementary material, the primordial presentations in which all subsequent psychical growth is generated.

Elementary presentations. The most elementary form of presentation, that from which Herbart considers the whole after-contents of the mind are built up, "is not an object with many properties, something in time or space, but simple qualities such as red, blue, sour, sweet, and not even a general concept of these, but just such a presentation as would arise out of a momentary comprehension of each quality through the senses."[2] If such elementary presentations are combined (as white, sweet, heavy, in sugar), a derived or compound presentation or "observation"[3] (*Anschauung*) is the result. The "observation," however, is invariably the presentation of a single thing: this oak, this beech. We have a particular presentation of each tree in our garden, but there is also a presentation valid for all (a concept). Such a presentation is general, abstract, while an "observation" is particular.

---

[1] Taken from Prof. Tyndall's Belfast address. Any adequate account of the remaining sense organs would occupy too much space here; the reader can refer for it to many excellent English works: Prof. Sully's *Human Mind*, Prof. Höffding's *Psychology*, etc.
[2] *Lehrbuch zur Psychologie Observation*, p. 10, J. F. Herbart.
[3] See note [2] on *Anschauung*, p 19.

We may therefore divide presentations into two classes, *i.e.* concrete and abstract, and the concrete again into two species, *i.e.* simple and compound.

Presentations the contents of the soul. Presentations form the contents of the soul. The term *contents*, as here used by Herbart, does not signify the entrance of something taken from the external world into the soul. As a consequence of the physical stimulus, a certain condition arises in the soul. The soul then is the bearer of the presentations which combine in it. **Identical presentations.** If, for instance, I see a tulip to-day and another to-morrow exactly like it, I have not two presentations of the tulip, but a single one, which is much clearer after the second view than after the first. Hence the law, *Identical presentations coalesce to form a single clear presentation.*

Analogous presentations. But all presentations are not identical. Many are only analogous; that is to say, they combine both identical and disparate elements. When I look at a square table and a rectangular table, all that is identical in the presentations combines and comes out clearly (four feet, plane surface). The disparate elements (square, rectangular forms) also struggle towards clearness; but they, unlike the identical, war against and, as it were, mutually suppress each other, while the identical mount to unchecked clearness. Hence the law of analogous presentations, *The identical elements promote, the disparate check, each other.*

In the identical we forget the disparate, or at least, if the disparate are to come out clearly, a certain degree of effort is needed. In other words, while we retain the class qualities of things, the accidents are apt to fall away, *i.e.* be forgotten. Mr. Galton, in his attempt to take a composite photograph of twelve criminals, found that by exposing the plate to each face one-twelfth of the time required for taking an ordinary photograph, he obtained one in which the characteristics common to all appeared, while the individual peculiarities were quite indistinct. Such a composite photograph does the mind take of presentations containing identical and disparate elements. Hence the law, *Analogous presentations blend with one another.* This blending takes place most readily when the presentations are made almost contemporaneously.

Disparate presentations. But there are also presentations which are entirely disparate, for instance heavy, white, sweet. Here no blending can take place, for *none* of the elements are identical. But if they enter consciousness at the same time, they form a group the elements of which belong together, as in sugar. In visiting a salt mine I *see* the miners, the excavations, etc., *hear* the rumbling of the trucks, *smell* the salt in the atmosphere and the close air of the mine, *taste* the water impregnated with salt in the lakes, and *touch* my neighbour's shoulder to guide me in the descent. These presentations together form what Herbart called the *complication* of a salt mine.

Rise and fall of presentations. If I look at a plant attentively, I think of nothing else; but if I am disturbed, the presentation of the plant disappears, making room for the presentation of the sound or sight, etc., which disturbed me. The first presentation is suppressed, checked; in Herbart's words, arrest has taken place: it has sunk down. Thereby he merely signifies that its clearness has gradually diminished, until at length I am no longer conscious of it. If the cause of disturbance be removed, I easily recollect the first presentation without looking at the plant. It grows clearer, again fills the whole of consciousness, and now the presentation made by the disturbing cause—sound, sight, etc.—has sunk. Herbart says that a presentation sinks when it is suppressed by another; it disappears for a time from consciousness, though not out of the mind itself, and rises again as opportunity offers. These two processes of rising and sinking constitute what Herbart calls the movement of presentations.[1] Accurately speaking, only a single presentation occupies the foreground of consciousness at any one time. The others, which have disappeared from it, are, as Herbart expresses it,

---

[1] *Science of Education*, p. 126.

below the threshold of consciousness, or are in the condition of sinking or rising. Hence we conceive of *the limits of consciousness*. The moment "when a presentation becomes a re-presentation—that is, when it rises out of a condition of complete suppression "—it is said by Herbart to be " on the threshold of consciousness."

The equilibrium of consciousness. The presentations are never all at rest; some are in a state of flux. In Herbart's words, " the mind is always in motion." Nevertheless, as he expresses it, the circle of thought is said to be at rest, in equilibrium, when no abnormal acceleration of the course of the presentations takes place, that is when there is a sufficiency of force among them to hold them equally in a condition of arrest.

Laws of the reproduction of presentations. The example given above shows that if a presentation has disappeared from consciousness, it can nevertheless return, be *reproduced*. This process of reproduction is governed by definite laws, first formulated by Aristotle.

Law of Contiguity. The most important of these laws is that of Contiguity, which may be thus expressed. Presentations which occur together or in immediate succession tend to cohere, so that the future appearance of any one of them tends to recall or suggest the others. Crœsus, King of Lydia, being condemned to be burned to death by his conqueror Cyrus, called aloud the name of Solon. The reverse of fortune he was then enduring recalled to him the time long before, when he, then in the height of his prosperity, was told by Solon he could not call him happy until his death, for great prosperity in this life was often followed by great misfortune. The endurance of this misfortune recalled the thought of him who had spoken of its possibility.

The law of Similarity. The second law is the law of Similarity. It may be thus expressed. A presentation tends to recall a past presentation or presentations when some of the elements in both are analogous. The greater the number of these analogous elements, and consequently the greater the similarity of the presentations, the stronger will be the force of the recall. Certain traits in the face of Duncan while he slept, recalled so vividly to Lady Macbeth the image of her father, that her intention to murder Duncan was arrested.

> " Had he not resembled
> My father as he slept, I had done't." [1]

The law of Contrast. The third law is the law of Contrast, which may be thus expressed: A presentation tends to recall a past presentation or presentations when almost all the elements in both are opposites. Columbus, in his old age, was unjustly cast into prison by his ungrateful sovereigns (Ferdinand and Isabella). On his release he hung his fetters in his room as symbols of the ingratitude of princes. Looking at them, he was reminded by contrast of the rich gifts he had before received for his services and of the former gratitude of his sovereigns. The law of contrast is, according to certain psychologists, of less importance than the other two, since calling up ideas by contrast is rather the result of a habit of thought acquired by the discrimination involved in perception, than an original tendency.[2]

Herbart, in his *Lehrbuch zur Psychologie*, gives no classification of the laws of association. He writes, " Psychological works are full of observations, which are not necessary here, about the association of presentations, the manner in which they recall one another, not merely by connections once perceived in space and time, but also by similarities, and apparently by contrasts." [3] This order of enumeration seems to

---

[1] *Macbeth*, Act II., Scene 2.
[2] " Kant was in express opposition to associationism, and to the extent that his influence prevailed, all such inquiries as the English associationists went on to prosecute were discounted in Germany. Notwithstanding, under the very shadow of his authority, a corresponding, if not related, movement was initiated by Herbart. Peculiar and widely different from anything conceived of by the associationists as Herbart's metaphysical opinions were, he was at one with them, and at variance with Kant in assigning fundamental importance to the psychological investigation of the development of consciousness, nor was his conception of the laws determining the interaction and flow of mental presentations and re-presentations, when taken in its bare psychological import, essentially different from theirs " (" Association of Ideas," *Encyclopædia Britannica*, by Prof. Croom Robertson).
[3] *Lehrbuch zur Psychologie*, Obs. 92.

indicate that he considered the law of contiguity," connections once perceived in space and time," the most important. The context may indicate, he held with earlier English psychologists, that the other two laws of similarity and contrast are reducible to the fundamental law of contiguity; but, at any rate, it is clear he held them to be of minor importance.[1]

Presentations indestructible. "We may almost say," writes Herbart, "there are no such things as destroyed presentations."[2] They are retained in the mind, merely becoming latent through the subduing power of other presentations. Thus, for example, "in travelling, where novelties of all kinds press in upon us, mental food is often supplied so rapidly from without that there is no time for digestion. We regret that the quickly shifting impressions can leave no permanent imprint. In reality, however, it is with this as with reading. How often we regret not being able to retain in the memory one-thousandth part of what is read. It is comforting in both cases to know that the seen as well as the read has made a mental impression."[3]

Immediate reproduction of presentations. The presentations are, as it were, elastic springs, which can be pressed down, but fly back to their original position as soon as the pressure is removed. When a presentation rises by virtue of its own force above the threshold of consciousness, what is called an *immediate reproduction* takes place. Herbart defines it as "that reproduction which by its own force follows upon the yielding of the hindrances. The ordinary case is that a presentation gained by a new act of perception presses back everything present in con-

---

[1] The classification used here is in accordance with Herbart, but not with Ufer, who gives a fourfold division in the following order: (1) law of similarity, (2) of contrast, (3) of co existence, (4) of sequence, thus subdividing the law of contiguity into co-existence and sequence. Prof. Höffding gives a threefold division as follows: (1) association of ideas by similarity; (2) association of ideas by the relation between the parts and the whole; (3) association of ideas by external connection (contiguity). He assigns the first place to the law of similarity on the ground that every association by contiguity presupposes an association of similarity, and he eventually reduces the three laws to one: the law of totality (*Psychology*, by Prof. Höffding, chap. v., "The Psychology of Cognition"). Prof. Sully gives the classification we have used here.

[2] *Lehrbuch zur Psychologie*, Obs. 11.
[3] *Life of Schopenhauer*, Helen Zimmern, p. 122.

sciousness opposed to the old presentation, which is similar to the new one. Then, without further difficulty, the old concept rises of itself."[1] A curious testimony to the mind's power of immediately reproducing, not only presentations in the form in which they have been acquired, but also after they have been unconsciously elaborated in the brain, was given by Prof. Helmholtz: "As I have often been in the uncomfortable state of being compelled to wait for 'happy thoughts,' I have gained some experience of how and when they came to me. Sometimes it was suddenly and without effort, like an inspiration. So far as my experience goes, they never come to the tired brain, nor at the desk. I was always obliged to turn my problem about on all sides, so that I could follow all its turns and windings in my head without writing. This involved long preparatory work. Then, after the fatigue caused thereby was over, I had to take an hour of bodily refreshment, and then the 'happy thoughts' came. Often when I woke up in the morning they were there."[2]

Immediate reproduction is of two kinds. In the first case, the thoughts with which we have been occupied, after disappearing, return of themselves, as on awaking from sleep or on returning to business after an interruption, when the presentations of the objects with which we have been occupied, having been suppressed for a time by some disturbing element, come back of themselves. In the second case, to take an example, a presentation A is suppressed by another, B; and a third, C, which will not fuse with B, enters from without. B and C contend with and check each other; the suppressed presentation A takes advantage of this, and again rises above the threshold of consciousness. Let, for instance, A signify the tone of a voice, B the seeing of a plant, C the hearing of a similar voice. B and C contend, check each other, and the older presentation of the voice rises into consciousness. The suppressed presentation regains its place through the mutual opposition of the others.

---

[1] *Lelrbuch zur Psychologie.* chap iii., p. 26.
[2] Speech by Prof. Helmholtz on h.s seventieth birthday.

Mediate reproduction of presentations. The opposite process to immediate, Herbart calls mediate reproduction. It takes place when a presentation brings back with it into consciousness another with which it was previously united. The former presentation is called an "assistant." Presentations which thus call up each other are said to be linked, *associated*. The associations which are formed of fused presentations are the most enduring. Of the "complications" before explained, where only an artificial connection exists, an element may easily be forgotten.

Passive and active reproduction. The power of reproduction varies in different individuals and in the same individuals at different times. The reproduction of presentations may be either passive, when the mind yields itself to the flow of its thoughts, or active, when by a *voluntary* use of the laws of association we recall past presentations. A humorous example of *passive reproduction* is Mr. Brooke's speech to the electors of Middlemarch. " Mr. Brooke having lost other clues, fell back on himself and his qualifications, always an appropriate, graceful subject for a candidate. ' I am a close neighbour of yours, my good friends; you've known me on the bench a good while; I've always gone a good deal into public questions—machinery now, and machine-breaking: you're many of you concerned with machinery, and I've been going into that lately. It won't do, you know, breaking machines; everything must go on: trade, manufactures, commerce, interchange of staples—that kind of thing—since Adam Smith—that must go on. We must look all over the globe—"observation with extensive view "—must look everywhere, "from China to Peru," as somebody says, Johnson, I think—" the *Rambler*," you know. That is what I have done up to a certain point—not as far as Peru, but I've not always stayed at home. I saw it wouldn't do. I've been in the Levant, where some of your Middlemarch goods go, and then again in the Baltic. The Baltic, now!'"[1]

The *active process* before mentioned into which the will enters, may be called recollection (*sich besinnen*). Schopen-

---

[1] *Middlemarch*, George Eliot, chap. li.

hauer describes this voluntary use of the laws of thought by himself: " If I faintly perceive an idea which looks like a dim picture before me, I am possessed with an ineffable longing to grasp it; I leave everything else and follow my idea through all its tortuous windings, as the huntsman follows the stag; I attack it from all sides, and hem it in until I seize it, make it clear, and having fully mastered it, embalm it on paper. Those ideas which I capture after many fruitless chases are generally the best."[1] The following is a concrete illustration of the voluntary use of the laws of association: "You ask me the name of the statesman who tried so hard to set poor Louis XVI.'s finances in order, and I cannot remember it. Not remembering the initial of the name, I let my mind dwell for a moment on Lous XVI. As I do so the names of Calonne, of La Fayette, even of Burke and Pitt, occur to me. These are not what I want, and I refuse to let my mind dwell on them. I think of Madame de Staël—stop! she was the daughter of the statesman whose name I seek. Of Gibbon; that reminds me that he had sought the same lady in marriage. Then Geneva, and Lausanne, and Ferney, and Voltaire, all names which are connected, come rapidly through my mind, and in the midst of them Necker's name is suggested, and I fasten on it at once. It is what I wanted." The voluntary effort here consists, as Mr. Fitch points out, in fixing the attention on the hopeful suggestions as they emerge, and withdrawing it from the rest.[2]

Definition of memory. Herbart defines memory as the power of the mind " to retain and reproduce presentations in the same form and order in which they were first received."[3] He distinguishes three kinds of memory, each corresponding with the nature of the material upon which it exercises itself.

Memory is of three kinds.

Rational memory. We can learn and remember materials between whose elements there is a fundamental connection, by fixing our attention when learning on this connection. For

---

[1] *Life of Schopenhauer*, Helen Zimmern, p. 49. [2] *Lectures on Teaching*, Mr. Fitch, p. 127. [3] *Lehrbuch zur Psychologie*, 29.

instance, the chief points of any well-known historical epoch easily recur to our minds, because of the relation of cause and effect between them. Take the rise of the Dutch republic. The cruel intolerance of Philip of Spain led to the formation of the famous band of patriots called *Les Gueux*. Their protest against the *establishment of the Inquisition* in Holland being disregarded, the *Dutch revolted*, and under *William of Orange* fought against the Spaniards until the *siege and relief of Leyden* practically ensured their independence, etc. We learn thus intelligently (*judicios*, from *judicium* = judgment). The first kind of memory, then, is the *judicious*, or rational.

Ingenious memory. But Herbart saw there was much material of knowledge between whose elements there is *no* essential connection, and in learning which some other aid must be adopted. I wish, for instance, to remember the treble spaces in music, and in connection with them I think of the word FACE, which immediately recurs with the thought of them, and suggests them to me in their order. Here there is no necessary, but merely an arbitrary, combination. This method of learning is called by Herbart artificial or ingenious, because through ingenuity connections are sought out between essentially different things. The second kind of memory, then, is the *ingenious*.

Mechanical memory. But again, Herbart points out, there is material which can be learned neither judiciously nor ingeniously, but only by continued repetition; for instance, the list of prepositions. By frequent repetition, the series is so completely fused together that the first word suggests the second, and so on, till the whole passes through our consciousness mechanically, that is without any effort of attention or intelligence. The third kind of memory is the *mechanical*.

Essentials of a good memory. In the school each class of memory is utilized. A good memory must possess many qualities. What is learned must be learned easily—the mind must be *acquisitive*; it must be retained—the mind must be *retentive*; it must be retained unaltered—the mind must be *exact*; what the mind contains must be easily reproduced at any moment—

it must be *ready*; and, lastly, it must be *well stored*. These qualities are seldom, if ever, combined. A high degree of acquisitiveness seems to exclude a high degree of retentiveness, for when a rapid fusing of presentations takes place, the process is not likely to be so perfect as when it proceeds more slowly. There is not time for the complete links of association to be formed, and cramming instead of learning is the result. A good memory is built up by bringing new presentations into fundamental union with the old; the new then are not merely an addition to the old, but interpenetrate them. If this is not done, the material is worthless. It is not governed by the laws of association, and speedily disappears from consciousness, because it has no points of attachment. Thus the first kind of memory is the most valuable. In learning we should carefully avoid the intrusion of foreign presentations between those to be learned, since the connection of the latter would be checked thereby. The high degree of self-control necessary to this is only gained by long-continued practice.

Suppressed presentations. A presentation which has become so obscured that it has been long below the level of consciousness, is said to be forgotten. But this is only a relative term, for when once a presentation has entered the mind it may reappear at any time; we can never know it has gone. Voluntary forgetfulness is almost an impossibility; hence the Greeks ascribed supernatural power to their mythical stream Lethe. An instance of the way in which an idea that has once passed through the mind, may be reproduced at however long an interval by suggestion, is given by Dr. Abercrombie: "A lady in the last stage of chronic disease was carried from London to a lodging in the country; there her infant daughter was taken to visit her, and after a short interview carried back to town. The lady died a few days after, and the daughter grew up without any recollection of her mother till she was of mature age. At this time she happened to be taken into the room in which her mother died without knowing it to have been so. She started on entering it, and when a friend who was with her asked the cause of her agitation, replied, 'I have a distinct impression of having been in this room before, and that a lady who lay in that corner and seemed very ill, leaned over me and wept.'"[1]

Abstract presentations. The transition from concrete to abstract presentations is made by numerous perceptions and revivals of percepts of similar things. A child who has seen only *one* table with a four-cornered surface has but an individual presentation, and can have no idea of any other table. If he sees one with a rounded surface, the presentation he already has is extended; it applies at least to two different shapes of furniture. Every new presentation of a different table widens his presentation of table as such; the latter is, however, no longer the presentation of a single object, but an abstraction applying to all the tables perceived, which, however, cannot itself be seen. The child has unconsciously dropped many unessential qualities (four-cornered, round, etc.), and has retained those which are identical. The result is not a pictorial re-presentation of *a* table, but a general or abstract re-presentation of those qualities which are common to a number of tables. This re-presentation may be further remodelled by later observations (of flower-tables, work-tables, etc.), when qualities before considered essential may be discarded. The earlier re-presentation then is imperfect in so far as it is not the result of observation of *all* kinds of tables, and also because the involuntary perception of the single table does not estimate with sufficient accuracy what is common to all the objects, and what not.

Psychical and logical concepts. A re-presentation of this nature is sometimes called by Herbart a *psychical concept*, and sometimes a *common image* (*Gemeinbild*). The term *recept*, used by English psychologists, exactly corresponds to Herbart's psychical concept, and marks off this class of re-presentations from the perfect concept. "It is an image formed out of a number of slightly dissimilar percepts corresponding to different members of a narrow concrete class." It contains both the essential and unessential qualities of a thing. To separate them—that is, to find the *logical concept*—we must

---

[1] *Intellectual Powers*, 5th Ed. p. 120.

first (to continue our example), know all kinds of tables, and, second, the qualities which are not general must be *designedly* separated. For instance, the important points of a table to us in practical life—its size, its form, number of feet, stability, material, etc.—all these are no part of the essence of a table, but this essence, that which belongs necessarily to every table, is—(*a*) that it has a horizontal surface; (*b*) that this is sufficiently supported on legs, or their equivalents; (*c*) that the purpose of the whole is for something to be done or laid on it. These three properties constitute the essence of table.

Logical and psychical concepts compared. It is obvious that to determine the concept of a thing correctly is not easy, yet if the definition is false or incomplete, and is nevertheless considered correct and as such made further use of, the contents of the whole structure of thought raised upon it will be false. Concepts of material objects are more easily formed than those of psychical objects, because the qualities of the latter are not capable of appealing to the senses. Concepts are merely something *thought*, not something existent in matter. Certain oaks, firs, etc., exist, but not that which is a tree and nothing beyond. The logical concept remains unchanged; the psychical fluctuates. The latter differs in different individuals; the former is the same in all. Further, the concepts which are formed designedly remain psychical, unless every object necessary to the formation of logical concepts be forthcoming. By far the greater number of our concepts are psychical.

The importance of forming an interconnected circle of thought. Presentations, if they are to fulfil the reason for which they are acquired—*i.e.*, to be turned to account—must reappear readily in consciousness. The teacher must be careful that they combine with each other, so that the circle of thought may be easily traversed from any point desired. Without this, even under favourable circumstances, groups of presentations will be formed which have no connection with each other. Then, since each group excludes the rest, the action and volition of the individual, growing as they do out of the presentations, are determined by the contents of the group which happens to fill consciousness. Certain phases of thought and action present themselves which last until the contents of the group are exhausted; then another, which may directly contradict the preceding one, takes its place. The character of Louis XI. of France illustrates this. When the one side of his character—his devotion to his own interests, combined with absence of any sense of moral obligation—was uppermost, its active expression was a succession of cruelties, perjuries, and suspicions; but the other side—his gross superstition and fear of death—when uppermost, prompted him to acts which modified or directly contradicted the former. Thus the murder of Galeotti the astrologer, planned by Louis, was promptly averted by the latter upon the sage's acute prediction, that the King's death would follow his own at an interval of twenty-four hours.[1]

Since, according to Herbart, character depends on stability of will, which will is formed by the circle of thought, it is obvious that a human being with isolated groups of presentations, will have what is called a weak character—one in which desires and will are continually changing. Hence the great fact, which Herbart insists must always determine and regulate the teacher's activity, that "those only wield the full power of education who know how to cultivate in the youthful soul a large circle of though* *closely connected in all its parts*, possessing the power of overcoming what is unfavourable in the environment and of dissolving and absorbing into itself all that is favourable."[2]

Analogous presentations. Presentations which approach an already accumulated store will stand either in *identical*, or *analogous*, or *disparate* relationship to its individual parts. Identical presentations, since, as we have seen,[3] they only make those already received clearer, add nothing intrinsically new to the existent store. Disparate presentations only admit of the arbitrary connection existent in a "complication."[4] Therefore we can only properly apply the term *apperception*, or assimilation, to *analogous* presentations.

---

[1] *Quentin Durward*, Sir Walter Scott, chap. xii.
[2] *Science of Education*, p. 92.   [3] P. 23.   [4] P. 24.

Apperception. Apperception re-forms both old and new presentations or groups of presentations. Sometimes the re-formation of the new depends on the character of the old. For instance, the old presentations supplied by Copernicus tell us the earth is a sphere revolving round the sun. Sight (or rather an incorrect inference from sight[1]) provides us with a new presentation, *i.e.*, that the earth is a plane round which the sun revolves. Nevertheless we do not believe our sight, and the new presentation it provides us with is re-formed by the old. In Prescott's *Conquest of Mexico* we are told that the Indians, who had never seen a horse until Cortes landed there, "believed the horse and his rider to be one and the same." This presentation was re-formed when, after a man and horse being killed, they found them to be separate entities. In this case, contrary to the last, the old was re-formed by the new presentation.

The process of apperception defined. *Apperception may be defined as that interaction of two analogous presentations or groups of presentations, whereby the one is more or less re-formed by the other, and ultimately fused with it.*[2] Every presentation (perception) is formed more or less under the co-operating and determining influence of apperception; that is to say, under the influence of the elements acquired by the mind's previous activity. Often, however, this is not sufficient for the complete mastery of the new; the links which connect

---

[1] "One of the most celebrated examples of a universal error produced by mistaking an inference for the direct evidence of the senses was the resistance made on the ground of common-sense to the Copernican system. People fancied they *saw* the sun rise and set, and the stars revolve in circles round the pole. We now know that they saw no such thing; what they really saw was a set of appearances equally reconcilable with the theory they held and with a totally different one" (*Fallacies of Observation Logic*, J. S. Mill). The student must bear in mind that the knowledge that the earth revolves round the sun and the incorrect inference that the sun revolves round the earth are both, according to Herbart, groups of presentations, although *derived* ones. See note, p. 11.

[2] "Apperception is that psychical activity by which individual perceptions, ideas, or idea complexes are brought into relation to our previous intellectual and emotional life, associated with it, and thus raised to greater clearness, activity, and significance" (*Apperception: a Monograph on Psychology and Pedagogy*, Karl Lange).

the new with the old in the act of perception are too few and too weak. But the connection *ought* to be as many-sided and as strong as possible, and therefore the perception must in many instances receive further thought, in consequence of which a renewed, more perfect, and stronger apperception takes place. To this end the teacher's or another's help is often necessary to call up in the child's mind presentations analogous to the new. "The teacher must explore the existing store of thoughts in the children." If all the old presentations capable of entering into the act of apperception " stood like armed men in the strongholds of consciousness, ready to hurl themselves upon everything that appeared at the portals of the senses, overcoming and making it serviceable to themselves,"[1] such help would be unnecessary. But as this is not so, analogous presentations or masses of presentations often remain stationary for a long time in consciousness, and only fuse when reproduced at the same time.

Attention necessary to apperception. If apperception is to be perfect, consciousness must be *concentrated* on the new in its relation to the old, on that which is to be apperceived or assimilated, so that everything foreign may be excluded, and only such presentations as are connected with the new be permitted, together with that new, to enter consciousness. An interconnected circle of thought does not exist in the little child or uninstructed man; therefore the power of concentration, and hence the process of apperception, is more or less imperfect and cannot take place unaided. For the apperceiving ideas, being disconnected, are necessarily isolated and weak. And these cannot rise when wanted into consciousness to meet and fuse with the new, nor can they suppress the ideas foreign to them and to those to be apperceived (the new), without the teacher's help. In short, the child and the uninstructed man cannot "concentrate their thoughts." In Herbart's words, " the thoughts have not learned to wait. On a given occasion all come forward (*i.e.* both the apperceiving ideas and those foreign to them); so many of them become excited by the threads of

---

[1] *Zur Lehre von den Sinnestäuschungen*, Lazurus, p. 14.

association, and so many come suddenly into consciousness. The new (the ideas to be apperceived) are wondered at, but left unconsidered. There is no rejection of what does not belong to them."[1] Hence this concentration or disposition of the consciousness to promote a further growth of the presentations, which Herbart calls *attention*, "cannot at first be brought at all to run in an even stream."[2] He classifies attention as *voluntary* or *involuntary*, that is, according as the will does or does not enter into its creation. Involuntary attention he subdivides into *primitive* and *apperceptive*.

Involuntary primitive attention.
If I hear a shot when absorbed in work, my thoughts vanish for the time, and I listen to it without willing to do so. If the children in a class are restless, and I hang a picture on the wall, they are quiet; without any special resolve on their part, they attend to the picture. These are cases of *involuntary primitive attention*, which always depends on the strength of the sensuous impression.

Involuntary apperceptive attention.
If a child in my room hears me reading aloud from a scientific book, he pays no attention; if I exchange it for a fairy tale, he does so directly. For the presentations the latter supplies are identical with, or related to, many already existing in his circle of thought. The attention no longer depends on the strength of a sensuous impression, but on the arousing of related presentations, which are the material for an apperception. For example, a cat lying on the hearthrug was observed to take no notice of a heavy fall of coals from the scuttle near her, but hearing faint sounds from the distant kitchen of a pestle and mortar, ran there at once. She had been in the habit when the meat was potted of receiving pieces of it. Here there was inattention to a strong sensuous impression (fall of coals) and attention to a weak one (pestle and mortar), because there was a relation between the physical stimulus and the psychical interest, *i.e.* in this case the presentations of eating. Where there is a relation of this nature a secondary kind of involuntary attention is aroused, which Herbart calls *involuntary apperceptive attention*.

---

[1] *Science of Education*, p. 138. [2] *Ibid.*, p. 139.

Absolutely unknown material then excites no apperceptive attention, because it finds no points of contact in the mind; perfectly known material may excite, but cannot hold, attention, because there is nothing new to apperceive. It is a happy mixture of the known and unknown which interests us the most. *Involuntary apperceptive attention is one of the most important factors in education.* With its assistance the new is assimilated without compulsion, and thus becomes an integral part of the circle of thought.

Voluntary apperceptive attention. Involuntary attention, however, is often in itself insufficient. Even when children show some interest in a subject, the teacher must often encourage them to collect their thoughts, so that in a series of physical experiments, for instance, they may not only look at them superficially, but may discover what they are intended to demonstrate. The child thus clears the way, as it were, *by an effort of his own will,* and the presentations already existent in consciousness which are related to the subject in hand, answering to this effort of will, stream forth to meet the new, strengthening and drawing it by their help into the centre of consciousness. This is *voluntary attention.* "It is chiefly necessary," says Herbart, "when uninteresting matter is to be committed to memory."¹ Ordinary teachers, however, he points out, make a more extensive use of it. Thinking only of the moment's lessons, they take little account of the presentations already existent in the pupil. Then when involuntary apperceptive attention, which they ought to have aroused by connecting the new with the old, fails, they try to excite voluntary attention by encouragement, threats, and punishment. It is *involuntary* apperceptive attention, however, says Herbart, which the true teacher will seek chiefly to arouse, and to which he will attach the greatest importance, for "the mere resolution of the scholar to be attentive creates no clear comprehension, and little co-ordination of what is learned; that resolution wavers continually, and often enough wearies the child."² Hence the necessity of connecting the new with the old, that

---

¹ Herbart, *Umriss pädagogischer Vorlesungen*, p. 81.   ² *Ibid.*, p. 79.

is, of arousing and securing involuntary apperceptive attention at the beginning of every lesson.

Importance of voluntary attention. Herbart is unquestionably right in considering involuntary apperceptive attention as a most important element to the child's acquirement of knowledge. In imparting that large amount of material which is at first necessarily uninteresting, but subsequently becomes interesting, the teacher, however, must arouse and greatly depend on voluntary attention. Its importance in this connection Herbart clearly saw, and while warning teachers that " that alone consumes mind and body which is pursued for a long time without interest," adds, " yet this does not take place so rapidly that we need fear having to conquer the first difficulties of what will soon arouse interest."[1] But another use of voluntary attention he does not seem to have sufficiently estimated, *i.e.* its direct moral value in training the will to exercise self-control. Locke saw and emphasized its moral influence thus: " Though other things are ill learned when the mind is either indisposed or otherwise taken up, yet it is of great moment and worth our endeavours to teach the mind to get the mastery over itself, and to be able upon choice to take itself off from the hot pursuit of one thing and set itself upon another with facility and delight. This is to be done in children by trying them sometimes when they are by laziness unbent, or by avocation bent another way, and endeavouring to make them buckle to the thing proposed."[2] German teachers also highly estimate its value in this aspect. "The child," says Bode, " if he would give this voluntary attention, must not allow himself to be disturbed by anything external, must concentrate his thoughts, and control their course. This is the road to self-control, the protection against that shallowness and desultoriness which destroys the moral life."[3]

Feeling, and desire. Presentations, which, as we have seen, are primary states of the soul, have their own secondary states, which Herbart classifies as feelings or desires.

---

[1] *Science of Education*, p. 257.   [2] *Thoughts on Education*, Locke.
[3] *Educational Problems in Elementary Schools*, Bode.

Origin of feelings. All action of presentations on each other is manifested either as mutual arrest or suppression (that is, partial or complete obscuration[1]), or as mutual combination (complication or blending), which is also mutual furtherance. Every feeling, whatever its nature, depends, according to Herbart, on this arrest or furtherance of the presentations.

But every arrest or furtherance of presentations does not necessarily generate feeling. If it were so, since new presentations continuously enter the soul, consciousness would be always occupied and disturbed by feelings, and clear comprehension of objects, accurate thought, or reflective act would be impossible. Experience proves that we are practically unconscious of slight or momentary suppression or furtherance of presentations. The second hearing of a lately told tale, the recognition of a person we often meet, the forgetting of a name, all take place in us without any appreciable tension.

Unpleasant feeling. Let us suppose the presentation (or mass of presentations) A is reproduced by another presentation, a, and comes in contact during the process with a conflicting presentation, X. Then A would be furthered in consciousness by a and checked by X, and this conflict would arouse an unpleasant feeling. To take concrete examples, series or masses of presentations struggle with each other when we cannot remember a name, a date, a quotation; the minor presentation aids (for instance, the first letter of a name) are not sufficiently strong to overcome the arrest and produce clearness, and an unpleasant feeling is the result. The same result follows when we wish to banish something from our thoughts and are reminded of it (perhaps by tactless questions or ill-timed condolence), or again when the clear current of our thought becomes confused, or the rapid flow of presentations is suddenly checked.

Pleasant feelings. But possibly other furthering presentations $a' a'' a'''$ may come to the aid of A, so that the conflicting presentation X is arrested or suppressed. Then the clearness

---

[1] P. 24.

of A increases; and the victory over the conflicting X makes itself known as a pleasant feeling, modified by the expenditure of power. A feeling of pleasure arises then when the pressure on a presentation is removed—for instance, when, after long and vain thought, we remember a forgotten and necessary date or unexpectedly find a missing object, or when an event we dreaded does not take place, or when a piece of work at first unsuccessful, ultimately succeeds.

Concrete example of pleasurable and painful feelings. A mother promises to take her child to a circus. Presentations obtained from a former visit are dwelt on for days before; all other presentations are comparatively suppressed. Just before starting, the child is naughty, and the mother says she will leave him behind. Immediately a violent conflict takes place in the child. The presentations already raised are too lively to sink immediately beneath the threshold of consciousness (be forgotten), while new ones absolutely irreconcilable with them (prohibition) rush in simultaneously. They check the further rise of the earlier presentations, and the result of the checking is a painful feeling, which expresses itself in crying. Then the unwise mother relents, and the child is told he may go. The suppressed presentations again rush upwards, because the force which suppressed them is removed, and the child laughs even while his eyes are filled with tears.

Herbart's definition of feeling. Herbart then defines a feeling as *the becoming conscious of a suppression or furtherance of the presentations which are at the time in consciousness*. Repression causes a feeling of pain, furtherance a feeling of pleasure. If pleasurable and painful feelings follow one another so rapidly that they cannot be distinguished from each other, mixed feelings or oscillations of feeling result.

As we have seen, much of this suppression and furtherance is too weak to be differentiated as pleasurable or painful; but since the furtherance, as a rule, outweighs the suppression, it causes only a feeling of vitality, which is really an obscure feeling of pleasure. This feeling of vitality is the threshold above which individual feelings must rise if they are to be distinguishable.

Feelings must be formed through the circle of thought. Feeling is thus, according to Herbart, no separate capacity, but the effect of the interaction of presentations. The strength and vigour of the feelings are in his psychology conditioned by the strength of the opposing or furthering presentations, that is by the extent of the arresting or furthering action of the presentations on each other. Hence follows an important principle in his system of education, *i.e.*, *that all working on the feelings must take place through the circle of thought.*

Feelings of pleasure and pain. Feelings are of all degrees of intensity, from the faintest tremor of like or dislike to the strongest feeling of pleasure or pain. Suppression of presentations which have resisted the movement of our strongest series of presentations for a length of time arouses the most intense feeling of pleasure, while the successful and continued action of such opposing presentations creates the most intense feeling of pain.

Herbart's distinction between sensations and feelings. The distinction Herbart draws psychologically between sensations (*Empfindungen*) and feelings (*Gefühle*) is utilized practically in his *Science of Education*. Sensations (which are the primordial presentations) are primary conditions of the soul dependent on the mere perception of organic stimulus (*whether of the sensitive or sensorial nerves*), and arise out of the interaction of body and soul. Feelings, on the contrary, are conditions which are not immediate products of nerve stimulus, but the result of acquired presentations meeting together in consciousness. They are derived states of the soul itself, for they arise out of the interaction of presentations. Sensations minister immediately to intelligence; they are the material from which the psychical life is constructed. Feelings, on the other hand, minister mediately to intelligence; they are not merely building material for further mental construction, but form an important part of the already partially completed structure. Sensations have a very slight effect, feelings, on the contrary, a most important influence, on character and disposition.

Herbart uses the term "sensation" in the following connections. First, as made use of by unskilful teachers, "they

Use of term "sensation" in the "Science of Education." dominate the sensations" (*Empfindungen*) "of the pupil, and, holding him by this bond, they unceasingly disturb the youthful character to such an extent that it can never know itself." He warns such teachers against one of two results: either "character, which is inner stability, can never form under such circumstances, or it does so remote from the observation and disturbing power of the teacher, who will be astonished in after-years, when this secret growth expresses itself, at the difference between the aim and result of education."[1] Again, he apparently uses the term "sensation" to express a passing psychical state in the following passage: "We cannot expect much from that working on the sensations" (*Empfindungen*) "by which mothers especially so often believe they are educating their children. All sensations are but passing modifications of the existing presentations; and when the modifying cause ceases, the circle of thought must return by itself to its old equilibrium. The only result I should expect from mere stimulation of sensibility would be a fatal blunting of the finer sensations."[2]

Ambiguity in the use of the term "sensation." Because Herbart does not always clearly maintain this distinction between sensation and feeling, passages like the foregoing are somewhat ambiguous, and leave a doubt whether the stimulation he condemns is that connected with mere sensation, or that which works on the wider sphere of feeling. For example, though the *feeling* of pain with which we hear of the death of a dear friend is obviously essentially different from the *sensation* of pain which we experience from a burn or cut, Herbart includes under the head of "feelings (*Gefühle*) which arise from the nature of that which is felt, such sensations (*Empfindungen*) of bodily pain as cutting, electric shock, toothache."[3] This, taken in connection with his principle that all working on the feelings must take place through the circle of thought, indicates that what he condemns in the **Its probable signification in connection with feeling.** foregoing passages as transitory in effect, and therefore useless as well as opposed to the formation of character, is *the stimulation of feelings directly*

---

[1] *Science of Education*, Introduction, p. 85. [2] *Ibid.*, p. 230.
[3] *Lehrbuch zur Psychologie*, par. 99.

arising out of sensations (*Empfindungen*). That feelings can be produced by sensations, and *vice versâ*, is obvious. A continuance of wet, dull weather causes an unpleasant feeling of melancholy, and the reappearance of the sun an agreeable one of gaiety. Bodily pain produces the feeling of oppression and lassitude, its cessation one of relief. The perception of worms, slime, dirty matter, causes the unpleasant feeling of disgust. Such feelings depend for their degree of strength more or less upon the presence and duration of the sensation. True feelings, on the contrary, those which the teacher must form and to which he must appeal, because they arise from the interaction of presentations, the abiding states of the soul, " are strong and enduring, and grow into the deepest recesses in the foundation of human character."[1] This direct formation of feeling by the circle of thought in Herbart's psychology gives an additional importance to the work of instruction, and increased force to his words, " In the culture of the circle of thought the chief part of education lies."[2]

Feelings classified as formal and qualitative. Feelings, as the result of the interaction of presentations, may be classified as — (I.) those whose origin depends on the *form* of the course the presentations take: these are called formal feelings; (II.) those whose character depends not on the course, but on the *contents*, of the presentations: these are called qualitative feelings. Under formal feelings are included expectation, hope, alarm, surprise, doubt, etc., under qualitative feelings those whose contents relate to truth, beauty, morality, and religion.

Formal feeling. To take first an example of formal feeling, *i.e.* expectation. I wish it may rain; previous perceptions have formed in me the following sequence of presentations : (1) oppressive warmth ; (2) clouded heavens in the distance ; (3) approach of the storm ; (4) thunder and lightning ; (5) rain. If I now perceive (1) the oppressive warmth, I reproduce the whole sequence of presentations. Since the first perception is identical with the first reproduced presentation, both unite to form one. The same process is repeated if the following mem-

---

[1] *Lehrbuch zur Psychologie*, par. 104. [2] *Science of Education*, p. 214.

bers of the reproduced sequence are confirmed by perceptions of the natural phenomena. The consequence is that the power of the foremost members of the older presentation sequence increases, whereby its course is accelerated, and the pressure of its single members to unite themselves with the corresponding member in the new increases with every succeeding member. The reproduction, which up to this point received confirmation and considerable aid from the new, now outstrips it, and represents to me the final member of the perception still to be made, that of rain (No. 5), which, it is assumed, will be identical with the reproduced final member (5), as, for instance, the first and second members of the perception (oppressive warmth and clouded heavens in the distance) were identical with the first and second members of the reproduced sequence. The sequence of presentations, however, runs out much more rapidly than the phenomena and the perception of them. *In thought* I have already reached the final member of the old sequence and of the new perceptions, while the perception itself is only being made, we will say, of the approach of the storm (No. 3). This throws me back to there produced presentation 3. In the interval, before the perception identical with the old member 4 (thunder and lightning) is made, I have once more in thought reached the final member of the perception (the fall of rain), and nevertheless must go back to No. 4. I am at this point in the earliest stage of *expectation, i.e.,* in suspense.

Expectation. We may apply the example up to this point to explain Herbart's somewhat obscure description of the process,[1] as follows: " Often the newly aroused presentation " (any of the reproduced presentations in the sequence which are not contemporaneous with the perception) " cannot come forth " (it is thrown back to an earlier presentation which *is* contemporaneous with the perception). " This is always the case when interest started from the observation of an external reality " (oppressive warmth), " and to this a fresh presentation attaches itself " (we will say the fall of rain), " as if the reality " (oppressive warmth) " moved in a certain manner " (in the sequence of

---

[1] *Science of Education,* Book II., chap. ii., 2.

the five stages). "So long as the reality" (the oppressive warmth) "delays presenting this progress" (through the five stages) " to the senses " (that perceptions may be made), "interest hovers in expectation."

Then follows release from suspense. If the last perception be identical with the last member of the reproduced sequence, there is no further hindrance. The presentation made by perception (of rain) unites with the reproduced presentation 5; the strengthened presentation rises unopposed, and I have the feeling of *contentment*. If, however, the clouds suddenly disperse before coming to rain, the presentation thus made, which is not to be repressed, conflicts with the contradictory one reproduced. The feeling of this repression is, according to Herbart, the feeling of disappointment.

Qualitative feelings. (2) *Qualitative feelings.*—They are classified, according to the relation of their contents to truth, beauty, morality, or religion, as intellectual, æsthetic, moral, or religious. As an illustration of Herbart's theory applied to sympathy, a qualitative feeling belonging to the moral group, take the following. In the *Tale of Two Cities*, Darnay, the husband of Lucie, is brought before the revolutionary tribunal and condemned to death. Sidney Carton, who loved and still loves Lucie, ponders over Darnay's almost certain death and the grief Lucie will feel at the loss of her beloved husband. Thereby the group of ideas connected with his own loss of Lucie is vividly reproduced in Carton's consciousness, and with it the feeling of grief which accompanied that loss. At this stage his feeling of grief is identical with, or at least similar to, that which Lucie would feel were her husband guillotined, for both spring from the same source—the loss of a beloved object —and he understands the grief Lucie would feel. He feels, through the reproduction of his own loss, the loss of another. He has the feeling of sympathy. But his sympathy does not stop at this point. It rises to its highest human expression— " Greater love hath no man than this, that a man lay down his life for his friend." He takes by stratagem Darnay's place for Lucie's sake, the thought of whom so fills his consciousness that all dread of his own fate is suppressed, and he can feel on his way to the scaffold, "It is a far, far better thing that I do than I have ever done; it is a far far better rest I go to, than I have ever known."[1]

The essential condition of sympathy is thus a similarity between the state of soul in one person and that in another or others. This state arises, according to Herbart, like all the feelings of this class, out of the internal action of a group of presentations having definite contents. He who has not to some extent the presentations which affect the sufferer cannot feel with him; he has not the material for apperceiving the feelings of another. Ruskin expresses Herbart's theory that the way to sympathy is through apperception when he writes, "Human nature is kind and generous, but it is narrow and blind, and can only with difficulty conceive anything but what it immediately sees and feels. People would instantly care for others as well as for themselves, if only they could imagine others as well as themselves."[2] When once created through apperception, Herbart shows that sympathy becomes in its turn a new and powerful apperceiving centre — a truth exquisitely expressed by George Eliot thus: "Let us be thankful that our sorrow lives in us as an indestructible force, only changing its form as forces do, and passing from pain into sympathy, the one poor word which includes all our best insight and our best love."[3]

Desires. Desires, the remaining class of the secondary states of soul, depend, like feelings, on the interactions of presentations. The class "includes wishes, instincts, and every species of longing."[4]

Example of desires. When Shylock the Jew, in Shakespeare's *Merchant of Venice*, is asked by Bassanio to lend the ducats to Antonio, the presentations which form for Shylock the "complication" of Antonio are called up into his consciousness. They are, for instance—(1) Antonio's religion—"He is a Christian"; (2) his habit, unlike Shylock's, in lending money—"He lends out money gratis"; (3) his hatred of Shylock's people—"He hates our sacred nation"; (4) his disgust at

---

[1] *Tale of Two Cities*, Dickens. [2] *Relation of Art to Morals*, John Ruskin.
[3] *Adam Bede*, chap. 1. [4] *Lehrbuch zur Psychologie*, 107.

Shylock's actions—" he rails on me, my bargains, and my well-won thrift, which he calls interest." Another presentation—a pleasurable one—formed at the same time as these, and now by the law of co-existence called with them into consciousness, is that " of feeding fat the ancient grudge I bear him "[1]—the presentation of revenge. This is far more obscure than the other four, and it struggles to become clearer. Since it cannot become so completely until it is realized, the presentation is hindered in attaining complete clearness. The longer Shylock talks with Bassanio and Antonio, the more does this pleasurable presentation of revenge struggle against the hindering presentations in his consciousness, *i.e.* those of Antonio's wealth, his reputation, the probability his argosies would return safely, etc. The pleasurable presentation "of feeding fat the ancient grudge I bear him " is in a condition of desire.

Definition of desire and aversion.
Desire—the positive form of it—may be defined, in Herbart's terms, as the becoming conscious of the struggle of a presentation, or mass of presentations, against hindering presentations in consciousness. Aversion, the negative form of desire, may be defined as the becoming conscious of the hindrances a presentation or mass of presentations offers to opposing presentations in consciousness.

Distinctions between desires and aversions.
Desire strives to attain to what is not yet present, aversion to remove (fend off, destroy) what is present and makes itself felt. The object of desire is something incomplete which needs completion, the object of aversion something forced upon the individual, against which the presentations act with more or less success. In desire, says Herbart, the presentation of the desired object is the strongest and liveliest; in aversion, the single presentation of the object of aversion is clearer than any one of the opposing presentations. In both desire and aversion, presentations struggle against each other. The object of both is satisfaction, only the mode of attaining it differs. In desire, the object is something with which we would fill our consciousness. "Come hither," is the expression of that inner attraction, the beckoning hand the sim-

---

[1] *Merchant of Venice*, Act II., Scene 3.

plest symbol of it. In aversion, the object is something which we wish should form no element of our consciousness. "Away with it!" is the expression of that inner repulsion, and the averting hand its simplest symbol.[1] Desire is satisfied when the desired presentation reaches unchecked clearness; aversion is satisfied when the detested presentation is suppressed, and with it the feeling of pain it created. With the increase of experience, aversions are changed more and more into positive desires for those means which have proved themselves opposing forces to the aversions.

Presentations not external objects, the objects of desire. The objects of desire are not external objects, but only presentations. Shylock longed to cut off the pound of flesh that his presentation of harming Antonio might become perfectly clear. Hence the subject proper of desire was not the pound of flesh, but the presentation of revenge; the flesh was only longed for as a means to an end, the essential means for bringing about an internal state. To the objection that if only presentations are desired, it is incomprehensible why so many desires remain unsatisfied, Herbart would answer, that if objects were desired no desire could be satisfied, because no object as such can enter the soul. The paradox that we already have the presentation for which we long, is solved in that we have not the presentation as we desire it, for we have merely a re-presentation when we long for a sensation, an obscure presentation when we desire a clear one.

Shylock, then, would have been satisfied when the rise of the presentation was aided by the cutting off of the pound of flesh, *i.e.* when the hindering presentations had been overcome. Desire, like feeling, has two stages: suspense and its relief. Suspense is greatest immediately before satisfaction; the desire of the thirsty man for relief is greatest when he puts the cup to his mouth.

Classification of desires. The classification of desires by the Herbartian school is based on the impulses which arouse them. These are either sensations and perceptions, or reproduced

---

[1] *Empirische Psychologie*, Dr. Drbal, p. 276.

presentations. Accordingly desires are either sensuous or intellectual. These classes, however, cannot be sharply defined. For a sensuous desire is often satisfied by reproduction (recollection or imagined presentations), and, on the other hand, an intellectual desire is satisfied by a sensation.[1]

Desire dependent on the presentations. Since desires depend, according to Herbart, on the interaction of presentations, desire for a thing of which we have no presentation is an impossibility. It may be urged, to take a simple instance, we desire to taste a dish unknown to us. But we only do so in so far as we assume it will raise certain presentations of taste we *already* have into complete clearness.

Desire leading to will. In this way all desire, depending as it does on the richness of the presentations, grows, like feeling, directly out of the circle of thought. It is a most important agent in the formation of character, since, under certain conditions considered hereafter, it generates will. Herbart's estimation of its importance in relation to will caused him in his earlier writings to set up the awakening of many desires[2] as the immediate aim of instruction—an aim which he exchanges in his later work, *The Science of Education*, for the awakening of many-sided interest. The seeming contradiction between this early choice of the awakening of desire as the aim of instruction and his later words, " It is inglorious to be absorbed by desires," is explained, when we remember he is in the second instance referring not to the whole region of desire, but to those sections of it which stop short, and never become will.

Desire differentiated from feeling. Herbart differentiates desire from feeling in that feeling is a phase, " a temporary modification, of the existing presentations,"[3] while desire is a movement through many such phases. The sections of this movement are feelings.[4] But he confesses " that the facts which we call feelings can only with the greatest difficulty be separated from those called desires and aversions."[5] He distinguishes between desire and interest in that "interest

---

[1] *Empirische Psychologie*, Dr. Drbal, p. 281.   [2] *Æsthetic Revelation of the World*, p. 67.   [3] *Science of Education*, p. 230.   [4] See Lindner's *Lehrbuch d. Empirische Psychologie*, 6th Ed., p. 167.   [5] *Lehrbuch zur Psychologie*, 97.

depends upon a present object, while desire strives towards something in the future."[1]

Distinction between desire and will. Herbart clearly marks the distinction he draws between desire and will, when he defines desire as mere self-inclination to an object, *without the assumption* that it will be reached.[2] Every volition involves desire, but not every desire is will; there is a large region of desire which does not issue in a complete volitional process. Shylock, when first asked by Bassanio to lend the ducats to Antonio, has the desire for revenge, but no means of compassing it; hence it seems impossible. The words, "*If* I can catch the villain on the hip, I *will* feed fat the ancient grudge I bear him," mark the course of the transition from desire to will. As the force of the *if* diminishes, the force of the *will* increases. When the process is complete, when the difficulties are so far overcome that Shylock " conquers the future in thought," and is almost certain of his revenge, desire has passed into will. It does so thus. At a later stage in his bargaining with Bassanio, he knows (or, as the event proves, thinks he knows) that if Antonio forfeits his bond, he will be in the power of the man who has granted it. If that power is to be Shylock's, he must take the risk that Antonio will pay the bond, and lend him the money. The following sequence is formed in Shylock's mind, which leads (in his case only apparently) to the attainment of his desire—(1) to conceal his hatred and lend the money; (2) to make the penalty of forfeiture a pound of flesh; (3) to exact the penalty. When the causal sequence comes to the aid of desire, will arises from it. "*Will, then, is a desire with the presumption that it will attain its object.*"[3] "Whoever says 'I will,' has already conquered for himself the future in thought."[4]

Desire passing into will. Whether, then, a desire passes into will depends, according to Herbart, upon whether the individual sees or thinks he can attain his object.[5] But it is not neces-

---

[1] *Science of Education*, p. 129.   [2] *Ibid.*, p. 211.
[3] *Lehrbuch zur Psychologie*, 223.   [4] *Science of Education*. p. 211.
[5] So also Pestalozzi, who says, as the result of his experience at Stanz, "Whatever awakens a child's powers, and enables him truly to say '*I can*'—all this he wills" (Pestalozzi's letter to Gessner).

sary, in order that desire may pass into will, that what is longed for should be *really* attainable, only that it should appear to be so (as with Shylock). The foolish child wills where the man only longs. The will of the inexperienced youth goes far beyond that of the man who has extensively tested his power of attaining what he desires. "Napoleon, when emperor, *willed*; when at St. Helena, he *desired*."[1]

[1] *Lehrbuch zur Psychologie*, 107.

CHAPTER II

ETHICS

Herbart's definition of ethics. ETHICS has been defined as the doctrine of human character,[1] and again as the doctrine of what ought to be so far as this depends on the voluntary action of individuals.[2] By using the term "individual" in the second definition, ethics is provisionally distinguished from politics, which seeks to determine the proper constitution and the right public conduct of governed societies. A definition of ethics as understood by Herbart must combine elements from both these definitions and may be stated thus: Ethics is the doctrine of human character so far as this depends on the voluntary action of individuals, both as individuals and as members of the State. In Herbart's conception, the morality of the individual will ought also to regulate every form of social life: the family, the community, the Church, and the State.

In considering human actions many appear to deserve disapprobation, others approbation; many appear to us as good, others as bad. On the other hand, there is a class of actions in regard to which our judgment as to their badness or goodness is not aroused. If the head of an axe flies from the handle in the carpenter's grasp, and kills some one near, it never occurs to us to call the carpenter a criminal, because the accident happens without (against) his will; if a rich man throws away a pair of shoes, and a poor one finds and rejoices over them, we do not praise the former, because it is without his will that the latter receives the benefit. These examples serve to illustrate the truth, *What is done without consciousness and without will is neither good nor bad, but is in its moral aspect indifferent.* Acts, on the contrary, done consciously and with will, are sub-

---

[1] *Types of Ethical Theory*, Dr. Martineau, p. 1.
[2] *Method of Ethics*, Prof. Sidgwick.

ject to moral judgment; so likewise is will, even if it is prevented from coming forth in action. We disapprove when we see the intention to do another harm; we approve when there is the will to do another good. The concept of will implies action whenever possible, otherwise, as Herbart points out, it is nothing but desire.[1]

The good will. Herbart defines the good will as "the steady resolution of a man to consider himself as an individual under the law which is universally binding."[2] In his system of ethics, as also in Kant's, it is the good will alone which has absolute value. Other things often characterized as good—intelligence, courage, wealth, power, honour—are but of relative worth. For they are, Herbart urges, only so many instruments of evil, if the will using them be bad. For him, as for Kant, "there is nothing in the whole world, or indeed out of it, of which we can conceive, which can be taken without limitation as good, except the good will."[3] This truth is echoed in our own tongue in George Eliot's poem "The Spanish Gipsy":—

"No good is certain but the steadfast mind,
The undivided will to seek the good."

We must next inquire in what the goodness of the will, according to Herbart, consists. What is absolutely good cannot be limited by the relatively good. Hence the goodness of the will resides entirely *in the nature of the willing*, not in any object such as happiness, conformity to nature, etc., to which its efforts may be directed. Again, its worth resides wholly in its intrinsic force, not in the extrinsic success or failure of that force when it has passed into action. "Even if it accomplishes nothing, it shines for itself as a jewel, whose worth is in itself."[4] Not the act, then, but the will is for Herbart the real object of ethical judgment. "The moral law, we may say, has to be expressed in the form, Be this, not Do this."[5] Far from estimating the goodness of the will by the extent of what it achieves, Herbart urges that the worth of its resultant acts

---

[1] *Science of Education*, p. 211. [2] *Æsthetic Revelation of the World*, p. 57.
[3] *Grundlegung zur Metaphysik der Sitten*, Ausg v. Kirchmann, section 110. [4] *Ibid.*, Kant, p. 11. [5] *Science of Ethics*, Obs. 4, p. 155.

must be measured by the purity of the will from which they spring. That Herbart's position is really true is evident from a very simple analysis. "The word 'action' is a word of complex meaning, taking in the whole process from the first stir of origination in the agent's mind to the last pulsation of visible effect in the world. James Mill is fond of laying out its elements into three stages: (1) the sentiments whence it springs; (2) the muscular movements in which it visibly consists; (3) the consequences in which it issues. Of these, cut off the first, and the other two lose all their moral quality; the muscular movement becomes a spasm or sleep-walking; the consequences become natural phenomena, pleasant, like fine weather, or terrible, like an incursion of wild beasts. But cut off the other two, and in reserving the first alone you save the moral quality entire; though paralysis should bar the passage into outer realization, and intercept the consequences at their birth, still the personal record contains a new act, if only the inner mandate has been issued. The moment which completes the mental antecedents touches the character with a clearer purity or a fresh stain, nor can any hindrance, by simply stopping execution, wipe out the light and shade; else would guilt return to innocence by being frustrated, and goodness go for nothing when it strives in vain."[1] This radical difference at once marks off Herbart's ethics from utilitarianism and eudemonism.

The formation of will by insight the work of education. From this his conception of the good will's inwardness, Herbart derives the aim of his system of education. "That aim is not by any means to develop a certain *external mode of action*, but rather *insight* together with corresponding *volition* in the mind of the pupil."[2] "That the ideas of the good and right in all their clearness and purity may become the essential objects of the will, that the innermost intrinsic contents of the character shall determine itself according to these ideas, putting back all arbitrary impulses—this, and nothing less, is the aim of moral culture."[3] Thus the formation of the good will which is the union of volition and

---

[1] *Types of Ethical Theory*, Dr. Martineau, vol. ii. p. 26.
[2] *Science of Education*, p. 111.   [3] *Ibid.*, p. 112.

insight, and through that the building up of "character which is inner stability"[1]—this, according to Herbart, is the work of education. The teacher therefore must studiously inquire into the source of will and the factors upon which its formation depends, that he may not leave the choice of the right means to chance.

The circle of thought as the source of will. Through the clear and convincing medium of his psychology, Herbart teaches that *the one and only source of will is the circle of thought*. From it the good and bad will alike proceed. "The circle of thought contains the store of that which by degrees can mount by the steps of interest to desire, and then by means of action to volition."[2]

The circle of thought being for Herbart the source alike of insight and will, he concludes that "in the culture of the circle of thought the main part of education lies."[3] If his theory be true, it at once substantiates the vast scope and importance of the teacher's work. For he has the great responsibility, during many succeeding years, of the formation of that circle, and through it at the same time a large share in the formation of his pupil's will.

Good and bad in Herbart's ethics are immutable contraries. That which is bad cannot be also good, and *vice versâ*. The theft of Benedict, Abbot of Peterborough, when he stole the relics of Thomas à Becket from Canterbury Cathedral, did not become good because he gave the relics to his own cathedral of Peterborough.[4] The well-known proverb that "the end justifies the means"—that the end can make the means good when they themselves are bad—is false. Brutus pleaded that—

"Pity to the general wrong of Rome
Hath done this deed on Cæsar."[5]

But even though his motive was absolutely pure—

"He only in a general honest thought
And common good to all made one of them"
[the conspirators][6]—

---

[1] *Science of Education*, p. 85.   [2] *Ibid.*, p. 213.   [3] *Ibid.*, p. 214.
[4] *Memorials of Canterbury*, Dean Stanley, p. 200.
[5] *Julius Cæsar*, Act III., Scene 1.   [6] *Ibid.*, Act V., Scene 5.

the means—"that great Julius bleed"—was not justified by the end—"for justice' sake."[1]

The two classes of motives which influence the will. Because good and bad are immutable contraries, it does not follow that a character containing bad traits has necessarily no good ones, nor that one containing good traits has therefore no bad ones. Character is a complex, and consequently can and does contain a mixture of good and bad. But for the single traits there is but one predicate. Jacob fed the hungry Esau because he thought it was to his advantage; the Samaritan cared for the man fallen among thieves without thought of advantage or of reward. These examples illustrate the two classes of motives, interested and disinterested, which determine the will. Action in whatever form, which proceeds from an interested motive, is in Herbart's ethics absolutely without moral worth. For it is prompted by the thought of good or evil consequences to its doer, and the will which accompanies it is not judged for its own sake, but for the sake of what it will achieve. Such action is at its best eudemonistic—that is, done to create a feeling of satisfaction—and easily passes into selfishness akin to Jacob's, a disposition to benefit one's self even at the expense of another. "He in whom it takes the form of forsaking evil from fear of an avenging God, or of doing good from hope of reward in a future life, is hardly even in the outer court of true morality."[2] "What we gain in disposition to right conduct, by the intermixture of Divine authority in motives to moral action, we lose in that action's moral worth."[3] Herbart here, as very frequently in his ethical doctrine, is in striking accord with Plato, who denies all character of goodness to actions done for the sake of extrinsic benefits, whether in this life or any other.[4]

---

[1] *Julius Cæsar*, Act IV., Scene 3.
[2] *The Relation between Religion and Morality*, Ballauf.
[3] *Religionsphilosophie*, Drobisch, p. 148.
[4] "If you dare a little to-day from the prospect otherwise of greater terror to-morrow, your very bravery expresses only fear; if you refrain from indulgence now that you may have a richer banquet hereafter, your very moderation is but greediness: and *that* can be no true virtue which thus illicitly sets its heart on the very things it professes to renounce, and secretly worships the idol it dethrones, but a mere slavish counterfeit of genuine goodness, whose attribute it is to stipulate for no

Only in actions prompted by the second class of motives—
the disinterested—can there, says Herbart, be any moral worth.
In the good Samaritan doing the good irrespective of consequences beneficial or harmful, to himself, we see the moral will
as Herbart and Kant conceived it. Its essence is expressed in
the latter's words, "It is not enough for the moral man that
his act is in harmony with the moral law; it must in addition
be done *for the sake* of that law."

The intuitive judgments. In their conception of the good will as the
absolute good, and in their principle that will
ought to be judged in consideration of its form alone, the
philosophies of Kant and Herbart are in entire agreement.
They differ in that which they assign as the basis of morality.
For Kant it is the categorical imperative, for Herbart the
intuitive judgments.

The categorical imperative, the command "Thou shalt," given
by reason to the will, is, says Kant, a universal law. Its uni-
versality constitutes it the basis of morality, and obedience or
disobedience to it forms the moral or immoral will. Herbart
rejects the categorical imperative as the basis of ethics, on the
ground of its derived origin. For he argues "Thou shalt" is
a command, and all command is will. All will is equal in
value; therefore no particular will as will is superior to any
other will, nor has any original right to command. On the
strength of this argument he relegates the categorical imperative to a secondary position, and his words "that it was a
mistake to begin ethics with the categorical imperative"[1] are
explained.

For it Herbart substitutes the intuitive judgments, which
he also calls æsthetic[2] judgments, as the basis of ethics. They

---

wages to personal appetite or desire, but accept the intrinsically good
for its own sake as the sterling coin, for which all else may fairly be
exchanged away" (Plato's *Republic*, quoted by Dr. Martineau in *Types
of Ethical Theory*, vol. i., p. 75).   [1] *Science of Education*, p. 206.

[2] The student must carefully note Herbart's peculiar use of the term
"æsthetic" when applying it to the intuitive judgments. He did not
mean to identify the beautiful with the good, nor in any way to imply
that the conception of the good is deduced from that of the beautiful.
As if to guard against any such misapprehension, he writes, "I assure
my contemporaries that what I call moral taste has nothing in common

are independent of the will, and can estimate its value, and while neither issuing a command nor enforcing their claims,[1] yet give to command its authority, to obedience its value, to duty its obligation.[2] They are judgments of approval or disapproval springing up involuntarily when will,[3] with or without action as its expression, is considered. Not until a later stage—*i.e.*, till the personality has yielded itself to them, and *itself* elevated them into commands from which ultimately a plan of life is formed[4]—do they acquire the nature of the categorical imperative.[5] The subject of these intuitive judgments, then, is the individual willing. That will, Herbart shows, is always in relationship, either to itself or to the wills of others. These relationships of will he found to be reducible to five; they arouse the intuitive judgments either of approval, or their contrary, of disapproval. The concepts formed by the mind of those relationships which arouse approving judgments constitute what Herbart calls the five practical (that is, moral) ideas. "From that which the involuntary judgment cannot help marking in an unqualified manner with approval or disapproval, the will takes law, the principle of order, and the object of its endeavours. That which was marked with involuntary approbation I call a practical idea."[6]

Before passing to the five relationships of will and the corresponding five practical ideas, the intuitive judgments, as existent in little children, may be briefly noticed.

Intuitive judgments in children. Intuitive judgments are undeveloped in the child, says Herbart, until called forth and exercised by the sight of good and evil acts. As soon as he acquires in the place of mere impulse the rudiments of a moral consciousness, he cannot help forming these judgments (on

---

with the fashionable talk of the present day, and, moreover, is just as far from confusing the good with the beautiful, after the manner of the Stoic maxim, 'Only the beautiful is good'" (*Science of Education*, p. 207). He extends the term "æsthetic" to the intuitive judgments, not because moral judgments and the judgments of art proper are in their nature identical, or in their origin one, but because they have certain properties in common; *i.e.*, both spring up involuntarily, independently, and cannot be proved.

[1] *Æsthetic Revelation of the World*, p. 64. [2] *Ibid.*, p. 63. [3] *Ibid.*, p. 66.
[4] *Ibid.*, p. 66. [5] *Science of Education*, p. 206. [6] *Ibid.*, p. 209.

individual actions to begin with) provided opportunity is offered to him by his environment.[1] At first mere feelings or general impressions (for the little child is only vaguely conscious of what is worthy of praise or blame) they are indefinite, and often lead astray. They must therefore be developed into logically cultivated and clearly pronounced judgments, for upon them greatly depends the formation of moral character, the great end of education.

That they may be thus developed, the child, under the guidance of parents and teacher, must learn to judge himself by having *first* seen and judged others, whom he meets with either in real life or in books. "The untroubled child," says Herbart, "ought not to feel his existence, that he may not make that existence the measure of the importance of that which is outside him. Then, it is to be hoped, the clear perception of moral right and wrong will be amongst the observations he makes in the same way, and as he looks at others in this respect he will look at himself; as the particular falls under the general, so will he find himself thrown under his own censorship. This is the natural beginning of moral culture, weak and uncertain in itself, but to be strengthened by instruction."[2] Herbart here applies to moral education a truth which Froebel constantly emphasizes and shows in action: that the child first becomes clear in his own feelings through the observation of external things.[3]

Ethical judgments developed by the relationships of the will.
Ethical judgment then can be trained and developed psychologically in the same way as judgments of art, the former through the observation by the individual of actions as expressions of will, the latter by a like observation of forms, colours, etc. The judgments of art treat of the relationships of tones, lines, colours, etc., the intuitive judgments of relationships of the will. As specimens of lines, colours, forms, cannot be judged individually, but only in their relationships to each other, so a will, which, as we shall hereafter see, has two sides, cannot

---

[1] *Æsthetic Revelation of the World*, p. 71. [2] *Science of Education*.
[3] See Froebel's *Mutter und Kose Lieder* (*Beckoning the Chickens*).

be judged alone, but only in the relationship of those two sides to each other, or in their relationship to the will of another or others. These additional resemblances strengthened the similarity[1] Herbart had already detected between the judgments of art and the intuitive judgments, and led him, in extending the term "æsthetic" to both, to define æsthetics as the doctrine of the morally as well as of the artistically beautiful. A relationship of will, then, requires at least *two* wills. These two wills may be existent (a) in one and the same individual, or (b) in two or more individuals. The first class contains two, the second class three kinds of volitional relationships, a total of *five relationships*; and as their expression there are *five moral* (called by Herbart also practical) *ideas*. The two in the first class are the ideas of *inner freedom* and of *perfection*; the three in the second class are the ideas of *benevolence*, of *right*, and of *equity*.

The five practical (moral) ideas.

The two wills in one person. The accumulated experience of all mankind from the earliest times proves that there exist two wills in each individual, one commanding, the other obeying or disobeying, as the case may be. These wills are often in conflict, the one inducing, warning, and forbidding, the other alluring by promise of pleasure or terrifying by fear of pain. This contest in the soul has been the theme of great poets and dramatists in all ages. It was experienced by St. Paul,[2] described by Wieland in *The Choice of Hercules*,[3] by Goethe in *Faust*,[4] by Tennyson, as he indicates, in his *Idylls of the*

---

[1] See note [2], p. 59.

[2] "The flesh lusteth against the Spirit, and the Spirit lusteth against the flesh, and they are at enmity one with another" (Gal. v. 17).

[3] "Zwei Seelen—ach ich fühl es so gewiss—
 Bekämpfen sich in meiner Brust
 Mit gleicher Kraft.
  Arete" (the goddess of virtue)
"Erröthe Hercules.
 Erröthe vor dir selbst. Die bessre Seele
 Bist Du. Sie ist allein dein wahres selbst;
 Wag es zu wollen, und der Sieg ist dein."

[4] "Zwei Seelen wohnen, ach! in meiner Brust,
 Die eine will sich von der andern trennen;
 Die eine hält, in derber Liebeslust
 Sich an die Welt, mit klammernden Organen;

King,[1] while the story of Christ's temptation in the wilderness is a poetical representation of the conflict in its highest form.

Objective and subjective wills. The two wills are defined by Herbart in the third book of the *Science of Education*, on moral strength of character, as the objective and subjective wills. The objective will, based on the natural desires, inclinations, and passions of the child, is unstable and impetuous, and is largely concerned with external things; the subjective or commanding will, based on the intuitive judgments (which the child passes first on others and then on himself), grows up parallel to the other will, till the slow "pressure which men call conscience"[2] rules, or should rule, the man. The adjustment by the individual of these two wills to each other supplies the idea of inner freedom (first moral idea).

The idea of inner freedom. *Inner freedom is harmony between the objective will, and the subjective will founded on insight.* It does not consist in a mere self-determination of the will, but in its determination under such independence of sensuous incitement as is bound up with dependence on the moral. This does not imply the annihilation of the objective will, but only its gradual subjection to the subjective, till ultimately the man always acts from the higher law. The will is only *free*, when it has passed from under the yoke of the lower desires and passions, to submit to the good and serve it in the future. We are not truly free when we would *will*, only when we would *will the right*. Herbart's idea of inner freedom—knowledge of the good, and *willing* submission to its guidance—finds its perfect expression in Christ's words, " Ye shall know the truth, and the truth shall make you free." In his teaching the subjective will is presented to men as the " will of God," and their subjection thereto as " the perfect life."

Die andre hebt gewaltsam sich vom Duft
Zu den Gefilden höher Ahnen " (*Faust*, first part).
 The parallelism here between Goethe and Wieland, his predecessor, whom he admired and extensively studied, is remarkable.
 [1] " Accept this old imperfect tale,
 Now old, and shadowing sense at war with soul,
 Rather than that grey thing "
 (*Idylls of the King*, Tennyson, Dedication to the Queen).
 [2] *Æsthetic Revelation of the World*, p. 66.

Like Christ, Herbart saw in his subjective will the will of God, not as a law imposed on men from without, but as the welling up of the Divine will within the soul, and with Christ he appeals directly to it.

A picture of inward conflict, of disharmony between the objective will, and the subjective will founded on insight, is given by Tennyson in the Cranmer of his *Queen Mary*. Cranmer having become a pervert from Protestantism to Roman Catholicism, was nevertheless sentenced to be burned by the Catholic queen. He cries in reference to his recantation,—

> "There be writings I have set abroad
> Against the truth I knew within my heart,
> Written from fear of death to save my life."

The subjective will of Cranmer, terrified by "the fear of death" set up by the objective will, was not free to follow "the truth" (moral insight) "he knew." But the hour came when he made himself free from that fear raised by the objective, and renouncing the writings, Cranmer now, in obedience to "the truth he knew,"--

> "As the helmsman at the helm
> Steers, ever looking to the happy haven
> Where he shall rest at night, moved
> To his death."

The idea of inner freedom has no place in the little child, for the terms of the relationship are as yet non-existent in him. He has not even the right insight which is the foundation of the commanding will, much less that will itself. "The mother's tender care, the father's kind seriousness, the relationship of the family, the order of the house"[1]—all this the child observes and *judges*. By such judgments he prepares himself to discern, and by obedience to those he honours prepares himself to obey the higher law of obedience—the idea of inner freedom. The promise in the child of that idea—of the growth of insight and of the gradual triumph of the subjective over that which ought to be subdued in the objective will—is sketched by George Eliot in her poem "The Brother and Sister":—

---

[1] *Æsthetic Revelation of the World*, p. 71.

"Thus boyish will the nobler mastery learned
Where inward vision over impulse reigns;
Widening its life with separate life discerned
A Like unlike, a Self that self restrains."

The idea of perfection. *The Idea of Perfection* (second moral idea).— The harmony between the will and right insight arouses our approval. Reuben, desiring to save Joseph, yielded to the insight his brothers avoided, and thus conformed to the idea of inner freedom; yet he was wanting. He had not the necessary *power* of will to oppose his brothers, and this want of energy of will arouses the disapproval of the intuitive judgment. The character of the Apostle Paul was the direct opposite of Reuben's. Not only were his will and his insight that the Gospel must be preached to the heathen at one, but he strained every nerve to realize this unity in action. Ever "passing over," he was constantly impelled by the one thought of the need to spread "the word" quickly, and his will to press forward to "those that sit in darkness" grew in strength with years. This "onward, ever onward," is the solution of his life. What is the relationship of will contained in it? This: *the obeying (objective) will strove to reach the strength of the commanding (subjective) will*, and in so doing expressed the idea of perfection. If the commanding will be expressed by 5, and the obeying will by 1, the latter is obviously weaker than the former. If, however, the obeying will reaches successively the degrees of strength expressed by 2, 3, 4, 5, its power at length equals that of the commanding will. The commanding will mounts a degree—to 6—and the obeying will follows it. The objective is thus ever striving to reach the strength of the subjective, and since the potentiality of strength in the subjective is unlimited, the power of the obeying will is so likewise. In other words, it strives to reach our ideal: "zum höchsten Dasein immerfort zu streben." [1] In the Dorothea of *Middlemarch*, the idea is shown in action as the motive power of the life. "She yearned towards the perfect right, that it might make a throne within her, and rule her errant will." [2] "She"

---

[1] *Faust*, Goethe, second part.
[2] *Middlemarch*, George Eliot, chap. lxxx., p. 585.

—the subjective will united with the good element in the objective—" yearned "—the idea of perfection—" to the perfect right"—the ideal—" her errant will "—the lower claims of the objective. As we rise nearer to the ideal, the nature of the latter is to mount higher.

"A man's reach should exceed his grasp,
Or what's a heaven for?"[1]

Thus, since the will seeks to attain its full strength, the individual is led to act more and more in accordance with the idea of perfection.

The ideas of inner freedom and of perfection, taken together to the exclusion of the ideas still to be considered, do not necessarily produce the moral will. The idea of inner freedom requires harmony of the will with insight, but if the insight errs in its conception of the good, it will lead the will astray. Again, the power of the will which the idea of perfection requires may arouse the approving judgment, while its direction and therefore its resultant acts will arouse disapproval. This is abundantly illustrated in history. " There is no instance on record of an ignorant man who, having good intentions and supreme power to enforce them, has not done far more evil than good." [2]

The two relationships of will already considered have been illustrated as existent in one individual, and, accurately speaking, they must be so. An individual, it is true, may try to make his will the copy of another and to reach it in strength, but in doing so, it is merely the prototype of his will, not that will itself, which is external to him. Therefore he still only illustrates the idea of inner freedom and of perfection. The remaining three moral ideas, on the other hand, must be sought for in the relationships between the wills of two different individuals.

The idea of benevolence. *The Idea of Benevolence* (third moral idea) *is the disinterested devotion of the individual will to the will (or the welfare) of another or others.* The story of Pestalozzi's life of devotion to humanity is almost as well known in

---

[1] *Andrea del Sarto*, Robert Browning.   [2] Buckle, *His'ory of Civilization*.

England as in his native land. To realize the great dream of
his life—to elevate the children of the poor by education—no
sacrifice was for him too heavy, no effort too great. Often reduced to extreme poverty and ill-health, rewarded by the con-
tempt and ingratitude of the people, the parents of the children
he loved and lived to help, he worked on, strong in the faith as
he tells us, that "a more fortunate posterity will take up the
thread of my hopes at the place where it is now broken." Of
his life with these little waifs and strays, "his children," he
writes, "I had about me neither family, friends, nor servants,
nothing but them. I was with them in sickness and in health,
and when they slept. We wept and smiled together. They
forgot the world and Stanz; they only knew that they were
with me, and I with them. It was from me that they received all that could do them good, soul and body. All needful
help, consolation, and instruction they received direct from me.
Their hands were in mine; my eyes were fixed on theirs. . . .
Many and many a time have I gone without a dinner, and eaten
in bitterness a dry crust of bread on the road, at a time when
even the poorest were seated around a table. All this I have
suffered, and am still suffering to-day" (Pestalozzi was then
fifty-five years old), "and with no other object than the realization of my plans for helping the poor."[1] This disinterested
devotion to the welfare of others arouses the instant approval
of the intuitive judgment. Pestalozzi, whose life had expressed
in action Herbart's idea of benevolence, gathered up towards
its close the very essence of that idea in these words: "I live
no longer for myself; I lose myself in the love of my brethren,
the children of my God."[2]

The contrary of the idea of benevolence—*i.e.*, the idea of
malevolence—arouses, on the other hand, the immediate disapproval of the intuitive judgment. Malevolence exists in its
most hateful form, when an individual, angered at another attaining that which is unattainable by himself, works against
him, not because he can gain what the other possesses, but be-

---

[1] *Life of Pestalozzi*, translated by R. Russell.
[2] *Memoir of Pestalozzi*, Dr. Biber, p. 467.

cause he desires to prevent that other from continuing in his possession. In this form the idea of malevolence exists in the Satan of *Paradise Lost*:—

"Sight hateful, sight tormenting; thus these two,
Imparadised in one another's arms,
The happier Eden, shall enjoy their fill
Of bliss on bliss; while I to hell am thrust,
Where neither joy nor love . . . Live while ye may,
Yet happy pair; enjoy, till I return,
Short pleasures, for long woes are to succeed."
(*Paradise Lost*, Book IV.)

Herbart identifies the idea of benevolence with "the absolute good which our religion calls love." Our greatest religious poet has done so also.[1] The idea forms a cardinal part of the creeds of Buddha [2] and Confucius,[3] and stands out prominently in the teaching of Jesus,[4] whose human life itself was the realization of perfect love.

In two somewhat obscure passages [5] Herbart treats of the part these ideas of perfection and benevolence ought to play in the relationships between the wills of teacher and pupil.

The idea of perfection, as he conceives it, contains three attributes: intension,[6] extension, and concentration of will. Herbart shows that there is little intension and still less concentration of will in the child, and therefore that extension of the will—that is its direction to a variety of objects—mainly occupies the efforts of both teacher and pupil. Such extension of the will over a variety of objects is, in other words, the forma-

---

[1] "Add love,
By name to come call'd charity, the soul
Of all the rest; then wilt thou not be loath
To leave this Paradise, but shalt possess
A paradise within thee, happier far."
(*Paradise Lost*, Book XII.)

[2] "Let the love that fills the mother's breast as she watches over her child animate all."

[3] "Do unto another what you would he should do unto you, and do not unto another what you would not should be done unto you. Thou only needest this law alone; it is the foundation and principle of all the rest."

[4] "Love one another, as Christ hath loved you." "Love your enemies; bless them that curse you; do good to them that hate you."

[5] *Science of Education*, pp. 109, 110.

[6] Herbart uses the term intension, and denotes by it energy of will.

tion of the many-sided interest, which is so powerful a factor in Herbart's system of education.

"The teacher must represent the future man in the boy; consequently the aims which the pupil will as an adult place before himself in the future, must be the present care of the teacher. He must prepare beforehand an inward facility for attaining them." In other words, the teacher must prepare the boy by the cultivation of his will to answer in its intension, extension, and concentration, to the demands his ideal will make upon him when a man.

"The objective of these aims as matter of mere choice has absolutely no interest for the teacher.[1] Only the *will* of the future man himself, and consequently the sum of the claims which he, in and with this will, will make on himself, is the object of the teacher's goodwill (benevolence); while the power, the initiative inclination, the activity, which the future man will have wherewith to meet these claims on himself, form for the teacher matter for consideration and judgment in accordance with the idea of perfection." That is to say, the teacher can and will measure the demands which the moral will, he is to help the boy to form in himself, will make upon him when he becomes a man. Then, inspired by goodwill (the idea of benevolence), he will, as its definition sets forth, " in disinterested devotion to the will of another," help the boy to accumulate, by his own active choice between good and ill and by his many-sided interest, that store of power which he (the teacher) sees will be demanded of him by the idea of perfection. It is a store which, in accordance with that idea, will increase in maturer years in proportion as it responds to the ever higher demands of insight enforced by the subjective will.

---

[1] "Whatever arts and requirements a young man may learn from a teacher for the mere sake of profit, are as indifferent to the educator as the colour he chooses for his coat" (*Science of Education*, p. 84). In the principle that the teacher should, in the interest of his pupil, choose the knowledge he gives for its power to form character, and not for its practical utility, Herbart and Froebel are at one. "It has an extremely injurious, weakening effect on a boy if he is early given an aim toward which to strive, a something foreign to and outside of himself to imitate, such as, for example, training for a certain profession, a certain sphere of action " (*Education of Man*, Froebel, section 22).

The idea of benevolence, like the idea of inner freedom, has no place in the mind of the little child. Sympathy with the joys and pains of those immediately surrounding him must prepare the way for its recognition and acceptance. Since fellow-feeling is only generated, to begin with, in a small circle, in the family and in the home that benevolence must be learned, which is afterwards to extend beyond them. "Let discipline see that children feel much with each other, that they are companions in joy and sorrow."[1] In the perfect family life Herbart sees "the most perfect earthly expression of the Divine."[2] With the knowledge born of cherished memories, George Eliot, in "The Brother and Sister," sketched the beauty and potency of this family life as Herbart conceived it, reflecting itself back upon and forming the inner life of the little child, and preparing room therein for the larger idea of benevolence.

> "Our mother bade us keep the trodden ways,
> Stroked down my tippet, set my brother's frill
> Then, with the benediction of her gaze,
> Clung to us less'ning, and pursued us still.
>
> "Those hours were seed to all my after-good;
> My infant gladness through eye, ear, and touch,
> Took easily as warmth a various food
> To nourish the sweet skill of loving much:
> And were another childhood world my share,
> I would be born a little sister there."

The idea of right. *The Idea of Right* (fourth moral idea).—Where two wills express themselves in action, the sphere of that action common to both, is the external world. It contains the objects which supply some of the needs of every human being, and it often happens that the wills of two individuals are fixed on the possession of the same object. This can take place, as Hobbes has shown in his *Leviathan*, (1) when man is in a state of nature, which is a state of war, and (2) when he is in a state of peace, "into which he enters from fear of death, from desire of such things as are necessary to commodious living, and from a hope by his industry to obtain

---

[1] *Science of Education*, p. 262.   [2] *Æsthetic Revelation of the World*, p. 71.

them." In the first state Herbart's idea of right could not exist. "Where there is no law there is no injustice, and where there is no right there can be no adherence to or deviation from it; it is consequent to the same condition that there be no propriety in dominion, no 'mine' and 'thine' distinct, but only that to be every man's that he can get, and for as long as he can keep it."[1]

In this state, if two wills were fixed on the same object, the strongest would obtain it. Force, and not the idea or law of right, would make the award. But in the second state—that of peace—man relinquishes this natural right, "that he shall take who has the power, and he shall keep who can," and is contented with so much liberty against other men, as he would like them to have against himself. "Reason suggesteth convenient articles of peace upon which men may be drawn to agreement."[2] These "articles of peace" supply Herbart's idea of right. For example, in the earliest form of English society of which we catch traces we learn, that "the homesteads of the freemen clustered round a moot-hill or round a sacred tree, where the whole community met to administer its own justice, and frame its own laws. Here the strife of farmer with farmer was settled, according to the customs (laws) of the settlement as its earldormen stated them."[3] These "customs" formed the norm which regulated the action of individual wills. When that norm was disregarded, strife broke out, as, for instance, when one man tried to extend his own boundary by encroaching on his neighbour's land. Such a strife of wills, whenever occurring, arouses the disapproval of the intuitive judgment. While the appointed boundaries were kept, each submitted himself to the idea of right, which is thus *the agreement of two or more wills expressed as a law to prevent strife.* Herbart takes as its motto, "To every man his own."[4]

The distinction between malevolence and maleficence or active strife is, that in the latter the one will would probably

---

[1] *Leviathan*, Hobbes, Part I. [2] *Ibid.*, Part I. [3] *Short History of the English People*, Green, chap. i. [4] *Science of Education*, p. 230.

never have come into collision with the other will but for the existence of some object desired by both, while in the former the desire to harm another is the sole incentive to action.

<small>The idea of equity.</small> *The Idea of Equity* (fifth moral idea) *is that the benefit or harm intentionally done by one will to another must be returned to the will which originated it, either in some form of recompense or punishment.* Herbart takes as its motto, "To every man what he deserves."[1] For example, when Christ healed the ten lepers, one returned to give Him thanks, while the remaining nine passed thanklessly on their way. The action of the former arouses a judgment of approval, of the latter disapproval. The kindness conferred on the lepers by the will of Christ, was returned by one in the form of gratitude, and unreturned by the remaining nine; hence a false relationship or preponderance of benefit on one side was created. Again, if one will seeks to harm another—for instance, to injure the honour of another—our judgment of disapproval is aroused, and only ceases when that injury returns in some form on its originator. Thus Arthur, measuring the extent of the wrong done to his honour by the unfaithfulness of Guinevere, given in return for his boundless trust in her, cries,—

> "Thou hast spoiled the purpose of my life;
> The loathsome opposite
> Of all my soul had d stined, did obtain,
> And all through thee.' [2]

The wrong, in accordance with the idea of equity, rolls back upon the Queen, and Arthur pronounces her deserved punishment:—

> "I shall never come again,
> . . . See thee no more."

But the idea of equity also requires the *true* adjustment of recompense or punishment, otherwise the approval of the intuitive judgment will cease, and even recoil. Here the idea of equity requires that the sins of time, however black, shall only

---

[1] *Science of Education*, p. 260.
[2] *Guinevere: Idylls of the King*, Tennyson.

be visited with the punishments of time, and Arthur, who, uttering the idea before, gave voice to its justice in condemnation, now pronounces its justice in mercy. Thinking of the time when the Queen shall pass—

"To where beyond these voices there is peace,"

he, the spotless knight,

"Who honoured his own word as if his God's,"

speaks thus:—

"Perchance, and so thou purify thy soul,
And so thou lean on our fair Father Christ,
Hereafter, in the world where all are pure,
*We two may meet before high God, and thou
Will spring to me and claim me thine.*"

The five ideas classified as formal or material. With this the series of the original practical ideas closes. The idea of perfection is termed formal, because it only relates to the form of the moral; those of benevolence, right, and equity, are material. Otherwise expressed, it may be said that corresponding to the material ideas, there are three virtues: love, righteousness, and justice. The idea of perfection registers their degrees of strength, while the idea of inner freedom is their necessary presumption.

The idea of perfection, as we have already seen, has its place in Herbart's system of education, as forming one relationship of will between teacher and pupil.[1] In dealing with moral strength of character he passes it over, because it is formal.[2] In the same book he combines the two ideas of right and equity under the term "rectitude," (*Rechtlichkeit*), and means by it conformity to a moral standard. For benevolence, (*Wohlwollen*) he sometimes substitutes goodness.[3]

The five ideas combined supply the concept of morality. The five ideas *taken in their totality* supply the concept of morality. Their due and relative proportion to each other, Herbart points out, must be strictly observed, for the sacrifice of one or

---

[1] *Science of Education*, p. 81.   [2] *Ibid.*, p. 210.   [3] *Ibid*, pp. 210, 259, 263.

more to the rest, disturbs the balance of a well-ordered life. For example, the idea of equity taken by itself would be the barbaric Levitical precept and law, "An eye for an eye and a tooth for a tooth." Only when the idea of benevolence tempers its rigour, when the idea of inner freedom determines the mode of its enforcement, the idea of right subordinates it to law, and the idea of perfection dictates its strength, does it determine the will towards morality. Herbart refers to a similar disturbance of balance when, the idea of benevolence being absent, the idea of inner freedom is dominant. "If the idea of benevolence is wanting, inner freedom will take pride in its coldness, and thereby with perfect justice will shock the warmhearted and benevolent."[1]

Duty based on the practical ideas. "In practical" (moral) "philosophy," says Herbart, "it is shown that duty is based upon practical" (moral) "ideas. These latter possess an eternal youth, and through this feature they become gradually separated from the class of wishes and enjoyments that grow weaker with time, and are recognized as the only unchangeable things which can answer the requirements of a law to the inner man. Besides, they bear in themselves the stamp of an inevitable decree, because a man positively cannot escape that judgment whose general form they indicate; hence in those practical ideas are to be found the necessary contents which must fill up the general form of self-legislation."[2]

The five derived ideas. From the five original, Herbart deduced five derivative ideas. They are the extension and application of the original ideas to society. The idea of right supplies through jurisprudence the idea of civil right, the idea of equity, that of penal right. From the idea of benevolence is derived that of an administrative system, for every member of society must contribute as much as possible to the welfare of the whole, that the State may be prosperous and well administered. The idea of perfection supplies that of a system of culture, wherein each member of society contributes his part towards the culture of the whole. Finally,

---

[1] *Science of Education*, p. 264. [2] *Lehrbuch zur Psychologie*, p. 233.

from the idea of inner freedom is derived that of an ideal society. It is the subordination of the individual to the collective will, the latter being determined by the moral ideas. To Herbart, as these sociological ideas prove, the State was no mere political body, whose power is to be limited to the administration of justice and defence of law and order etc., but is a corporation which by its benevolent administration, its furtherance of moral culture, its protection of individual freedom consistent with social order, and its elevation of the general tone of the community, should make itself felt as a moral force.

Virtue, according to Herbart, is the perfect harmony of character with all the moral ideas. If a will is not subject to them spontaneously, but requires to be attracted to them, the concept of duty or law is formed. For an absolutely holy will, there is neither law nor duty.

Ethics in relation to religion. It is often maintained that ethics are based on the doctrines of religion, and therefore do not form an independent science. This cannot be too strongly combated.[1] But, on the other hand, it must be allowed that religion plays a most important part in the development of moral character. He who does the good only from the fear or hope of a future life is certainly far from being truly moral; but he who accustoms himself to withstand the desires of the moment, and to consider and hearken to the claims of the ideal, may ultimately become obedient to those demands for the sake alone of their intrinsic worth. "As the child's blind obedience to the teacher's and parent's authority forms a necessary stepping-stone to true morality, so humanity is led to the same end, by regarding the obligations of the moral ideas as the commandments of a law-giver feared at first, but ultimately loved above all. The way to morality goes, with but few exceptions, only through law." [2]

Religion needful to morality. Even when a higher stage of moral culture has been reached, man cannot live without the support

---

[1] " There are many religions, but there is only one morality, which has been, is, and must be for ever, an instinct in the hearts of all civilized men " (*Relation of Art to Religion*, John Ruskin).   [2] Ballauf.

of religion. He is to will the good, but willing, as we have seen, is only possible when success appears attainable. Without this presumption, confident action is impossible, for energy is paralyzed by the fear of failure. In the many instances then where success seems doubtful, human will to compass the good would be impossible unless it possessed a motive power beyond itself: faith in "the assistance of the highest Being, whose wise purposes are so ordered, that the good shall reign in us and in society."

Herbart's conception of religion. The whole tone of Herbart's life and work proves, that God immanent in nature was to him the great reality. Religion as the relation of man to his Creator, as the effort of the human soul to approach God, made up for him the great central fact of history, the illuminating light in which he interpreted the past, lived in the present, and gathered hope for the future. "God, the Father of men and Lord of the world," he writes, "must fill the background of memory. His must be an immovable place amongst the earliest thoughts [1] on which the personality of the growing man fastens." [2] Hence he attaches supreme importance to the cultivation of the religious spirit in the little child. "Religion will never occupy that tranquil place in the depths of the heart which it ought to possess, if its fundamental ideas are not among the earliest which belong to recollection, if it is not bound up and blended with all which changing life leaves behind in the centre of the personality." [3] The most favourable conditions to its perfect growth are to be found, says Herbart, not in the school, but in the home. On the use of religious instruction he writes, "Education must look upon religion not as objective, but as subjective. Religion befriends

---

[1] Compare Froebel: "Genuine, true, living religion, abiding in danger and in combat, in oppression and in need, in pleasure and in joy, must come to man in infancy. . . . Religiousness, fervid living in God and with God in all conditions and circumstances of life, which does not thus grow up from childhood with man, is later only with extreme difficulty raised to full vigorous life; while, on the contrary, a religious sense thus germinated and fostered amid all the storms and dangers of life will gain the victory" (*Education of Man*, p. 16). [2] *Æsthetic Revelation of the World*, p. 72. [3] *Science of Education*, p. 179.

and protects; nevertheless it must not be given to the child too circumstantially. Its work must be *directing* rather than *teaching*; it must never exhaust susceptibility, and therefore, above all, must not be prematurely made use of. Nor must it be given dogmatically to arouse doubt, but in union with knowledge of nature and the repression of egotism.[1] It must ever *point* beyond, but never *instruct* beyond the bounds of knowledge, for then the paradox would follow that instruction knows what it does not know."[2] His conviction that such teaching could be but imperfectly given within the narrow and unsatisfactory limits of school lessons, he expresses in the following words: (in reading them we are almost forced to the conclusion, that the modern Herbartian school, in assigning to the objective lesson in religion the central place in its scheme of instruction, has departed from the spirit of its founder) "Manifold as may be the resting-places of diverse minds, simple enough is that which should be the resting-place of them all: religion. But here your society appears to be led to a false conclusion. It says, much too small a place is assigned to religious instruction; that means much too little time: it is only looked upon as a secondary study. But it does not follow that that to which little time is assigned is necessarily considered as a secondary study, and will be treated as such. How would it be if the size of the place assigned the goods and chattels in a house were determined by their value? How large a space must the jewellery then fill. But the precious stones would refuse to take it; it is their nature to concentrate their great worth in a very little space. I cannot otherwise judge of religion. I know and acknowledge that it must form the deepest foundation and one of the earliest beginnings of human, even of child culture, without which all else is vain. I do not say this to-day for the first time; I said it in the first of my educational writings, and, if I am not mistaken, often and emphatically enough. But I am alarmed at a religious instruction which stretches out into a multitude

---

[1] For Herbart's thoughts on the direction of religious growth at a later stage see *Science of Education*, p. 162.
[2] *Aphorismen zur Pädayogik.*

of special lessons, just as alarmed as at an extended formula of belief, which sets forth in many articles how the heart of man is to approach the Divine. And for a long time I have been frightened at the modern recommendations of religion, which very visibly have their origin in the misfortunes and miseries of late years. Amidst these miseries, we seem to have forgotten all which knowledge of humanity, the history of the Church, the history of philosophy, combine to teach,[1] namely, that every ladder towards heaven with accurately numbered rungs, which are to be mounted methodically one after the other, is useless to satisfy the universal need of religion. Further, the genuine professors of religion have often extremely few articles of belief, and those who search most diligently declare, that what we know of religion, what consequently we can in the true sense learn and teach, contracts itself into a few very simple supporting principles of a reasonable belief. These are my conclusions."[2]

Religion in its relation to the child. Religion then, as Herbart conceived it, is to be in the main to the little child, not the nourishment of occasional lessons given to him like his meals at stated times, but as the air he breathes. It is to be, as it were, an atmosphere, quiet, penetrating, all-pervading, as necessary to his higher existence as the air to his bodily life, and almost as unconsciously received. In the midst of the family life,[3] "that which in the whole visible world is the most

---

[1] Written at the close of the Napoleonic wars.
[2] Notes on an educational essay read before the Society of Teachers, June. 1814.
[3] On the influence of the family life on the child, compare Froebel with Herbart. "Family life," says the former, "you are the sanctuary of humanity; you are the most holy thing there is for the care of all that is Divine. Without you what are altar and Church? What are they, when you do not consecrate them and raise soul, heart, disposition and mind, idea and thought, action and life, in all your members to the altar and temple of the one living God, to the awed understanding of all His manifestations, and to the carrying out of their demands?" (*Mutter und Kose Lieder*, Picture 16). Herbart, while duly estimating the mighty influence of parents over their children, leaves unnoticed the extent and significance of that which parents in their turn receive from their children. He does not seem to have recognized that *reciprocity* of the relationship which Froebel saw and emphasized thus: "Fathers, parents, come let our children

beautiful and most worthy," the child should picture Providence in the image of his parents, and from them idealized he would learn the attributes of the Deity. As long as possible the religious feeling, which ought from the earliest years to depend on the *single* thought Providence, must be preserved undisturbed. Herbart saw keenly the danger lurking for a child in too much direct religious teaching and too many religious exercises, *i.e.*, that " they tended to make the idea of God wearisome to him," so that in after-years, when the man needed that idea in its full vitality for his safety in the storms of life, it would be no longer unspoiled. From the perfect family life, Herbart taught there was but one step upwards possible : to God; and this step for the little child should be chiefly made through the indirect discipline of daily loving duty, fulfilled under the father's kind authority and the mother's tender care. Later, when many-sided culture has aroused inquiry, the boy and youth must be shown "the fruitless attempts of mature minds at all times to find fixed doctrines in religion."[1] In the " order of the world becoming ever more apparent to the growing mind, in the history of the race, in the whole of human destiny," not in isolated epochs of action or of faith, and in " the slow pressure of his own intuitive judgment which men call conscience," the boy must be led to search for and find the Divine.

---

supply us with what we lack. The all-vivifying, all-forming power of child-life that we no longer possess, let us receive again from them. Let us learn from our children ; let us live with them : so shall their lives bring peace and joy to us ; so shall we begin to be and to become wise " (*Education of Man*, Froebel, section 42).

[1] *Science of Education*, p. 162.

CHAPTER III

PRACTICAL PEDAGOGY

SECTION I.—THEORY OF INSTRUCTION

The formation of character the aim of education. The aim of education, as before explained, is contained for Herbart in the one word "morality." Its whole work is to form a character which, in the battle of life, shall stand unmoved, not through the strength of its external action, but on the firm and enduring foundation of its moral insight and enlightened will. " Since morality has its place singly and only in individual volition, founded on right insight, it follows of itself first and foremost, that the work of moral education is not to develop a certain external mode of action, but rather insight, together with proportionate volition in the pupil." [1]

Herbart then claims the formation of will, which is synonymous with formation of character, as the highest aim of education, to the attainment of which all its efforts must be directed. In the *Science of Education*, however, this the fundamental thought of the book is not treated of at first. It is merely stated *as* aim, and then Herbart passes on to consider the means by which it is to be attained, reserving any more detailed analysis of the direct formation of character itself, until the fourth chapter of the third book. He probably adopted this mode of arrangement, because he considered teachers required at the very beginning " a bird's-eye view of the means at their disposal." But he carefully guards his readers against being misled by it. As if to remind them that the aim was the one and all-important thing, and the value of the means consisted solely in their power to secure it, he asks those who

---

[1] *Science of Education*, p. 111.

have read the book from beginning to end to re-read it from *end to beginning*, when formation of character will have its true place of precedence.

The sequence of government, instruction, and discipline as means of education. The means which education has at its disposal to secure this aim are, in the sequence given by Herbart, as follows: government, instruction, and discipline. We shall, in accordance with Herbart's expressed views, first examine his theory of instruction, and then, that their natures may be perceived more clearly through contrast with each other, consider government and discipline together. "For the same reason," says Herbart, "that in psychology presentations were treated of before desire and will, in pedagogy the theory of instruction must precede that of discipline." Just as presentations must first supply the material from which desire and will are formed, instruction must first supply the circle of thought upon and through which discipline is to act. This in no sense means, that discipline is not to become active till the work of instruction is finished. It must move by the side of instruction, guiding and helping the pupil to employ the contents of the circle of thought which instruction supplies, in the service of the moral ideas.

INSTRUCTION.

Educative instruction. We have seen that one of Herbart's fundamental principles is, "The worth of a man consists not in what he knows, but in how he wills." True to it, he considers knowledge and that which provides it—instruction—only as means to a clearly defined aim, the formation of a vigorous and enlightened will. Any other kind of instruction or knowledge is comparatively valueless. "I do not," he says, "acknowledge any instruction which does not educate. Into what is learned for the sake of gain, or advancement, or amusement, the question does not enter, whether the pupil is better for it. Of such instruction I do not speak. I treat only of *educative* instruction."[1] Educative instruction, an expression originated by Herbart, has been well defined as instruction that makes for character.

---

[1] *Umriss pädagogischer Vorlesungen*, 57.

Experience and intercourse as teaching the child before school years. The child, when he passes into the teacher's hand, has already accumulated a vast store of ideas. In his early years " he gets acquainted with the thousand things of home, street, garden, field, wood, the wonders of the heavens, the manifold events of nature, the land and people of the neighbourhood, and learns to call most of them by name; he learns to use a great part of the vocabulary of his mother-tongue and its most important forms of word and sentence; he learns to think in the vernacular."[1] In a word, he *looks at* the world around him. In Herbart's language, he gathers *experience*. Again, from father and mother in their relation to himself and to each other, he learns the nature of home, and something of the meaning of love and duty. He comes in contact with brothers, sisters, and playmates, is happy or sad with them. He even extends these feelings to inanimate objects, believing they are living: he will comfort the sick doll, and pity the crushed flower. He *feels with* his little world. In Herbart's language, he has *intercourse* with human beings. "From nature," he says, "man attains to knowledge through experience, and to sympathy through intercourse."[2]

The child's store of thought to be examined. If experience and intercourse are thus actively filling the child's mind, what work is left for the teacher? His first step must be to examine the existing store of thoughts in the child.

This is necessary, firstly, that he may gather together and arrange the knowledge the child already possesses in such a way, that it may be ready to assimilate and be assimilated with the new knowledge offered to him in instruction. The mental treasure the child takes to school—those vivid ideas acquired by repeated sense perceptions during the most impressionable years of his life—ought to stand in the closest, most vital relation to all his later culture. It must form the firm foundation of the new instruction and be built into its structure, if the child's store of thought is to be, what Herbart requires it, interconnected in all its parts. Therefore what the teacher gives must be supplementing, never suppressive.

---

[1] *On Apperception*, Lange.   [2] *Science of Education*, p. 186.

"He has to reach down with regulative hand into those quiet private thoughts and feelings of the child, in which lie his *ego* and his whole future, that they may rise above the threshold of consciousness, and communicate understanding, clearness, warmth, and life to instruction." [1]

It is necessary, secondly, in order that the teacher may learn where the existing store is defective, confused, or incomplete, so that he may by instruction explain, correct, and fill up wherever necessary. "As we know that the child on entering school has mastered a limited part of his surroundings, and that many of his home observations need clearing up and sifting, we lead him back into the old familiar world in which he has heretofore lived, and which is dear to him. We teach him to know it better, to make him more familiar with it, and thus develop knowledge of the home environment."

Lange, in the same strikingly clear and attractive book, points out the incompleteness as well as the vitality of the knowledge the child already possesses. It is relatively rich in sense percepts, but one-sided, because it only covers a few fields. While there is a comparative wealth of such percepts, their very strength is a cause of imperfection, and often of superficiality. The child is so absorbed in one or two striking characteristics of an attractive object, that he has no attention left to observe the remainder. He thus obtains an incomplete picture of the whole. Herbart alludes to the general deficiencies of this knowledge in these words: "The gaps left by intercourse in the little sphere of feeling, and those left by experience in the larger circle of knowledge, are for us almost equally great, and in the former, as in the latter, completion by instruction must be welcome." [2]

The child's experience and intercourse arranged and amplified. All then that the child has already gained through contact with nature, (in Herbart's language, the harvest of experience) requires to be examined, arranged, and amplified by the teacher, that it may be used as the starting-point to a wider knowledge. All fellow-feeling already developed in the limited sphere of home,

---

[1] *On Apperception*, Lange, p. 106. [2] *Science of Education*, p. 136.

through contact with fellow-creatures — parents, brothers, sisters, friends (in Herbart's language, the gains of intercourse) —requires likewise the guiding, expanding aid of instruction, that it may be made the starting-point to a wider sympathy. In Herbart's words, "whenever a plan of instruction has to be made for any individual, there will always be found an existent circle of intercourse and experience, in which that individual is placed. This circle is capable of being judiciously widened, or its contents may be more thoroughly examined; this is the first thing which requires attention."[1]

Presentative instruction depends on apperception. At first this store must be used by the teacher as the basis of what Herbart calls presentative instruction—that which begins before the child can read, and which reaches him through directed observation, the teacher's descriptive skill, and pictures. Presentative instruction can only be understood and appropriated—that is, *apperceived*—by the child under two conditions: first, that it is related to groups of ideas already existent in the child's mind; second, that it is connected with and explained in the light of these older ideas by the teacher. We have seen that the experience and intercourse of the child's early years supply a wealth of such ideas. Both conditions then are fulfilled, if the teacher has the skill to call them up into consciousness and to connect the old with the new, so that the old can make the new, on the strength of their kinship, a vital part of themselves. This is expressed by Herbart thus: "From the horizon which bounds the eye, we can take measurements by which, through descriptions of the next-lying territory, that horizon can be enlarged. The child may be led back by the life thread of older persons surrounding it; we can generally render perceptible to the senses through mere presentation everything *sufficiently similar to and bound up with what the child till then has observed.*"[2]

Experience and intercourse used throughout instruction. But this fund of home observation is not to be looked upon as exhausted in the first months at school. Experience and intercourse are "the two

---

[1] *Science of Education*, p. 154. [2] *Ibid.*, p. 137.

constant teachers of men." They are an essential factor as an aid to apperception in almost every subject of instruction, and ought to be made use of during the whole of school life. Herbart thus estimates their immense value to the teacher as continuous aids: "Who can dispense with experience and intercourse in education? To do so would be to dispense with daylight and content ourselves with candle-light. Fulness, strength, individual definiteness in all our presentations, practice in the application of the general, contact with the real, with the country and the age, patience with men as they are —all this must be derived from those original sources of mental life." [1]

The two lines of instruction. Starting from presentative instruction, education, according to Herbart, takes two main lines: (1) the *historical*, which includes history religious and profane, literature, languages, and art; (2) the *natural scientific*, which includes geography, mathematics, and natural history, etc. In what way can these subjects be related to the material of experience and intercourse? How can it be used in later instruction? Herbart's detailed answer to these questions will be found in his chapters on "The Course of Instruction," and only the following short extracts can be given here, as illustrating his ideas concerning the early use of this material analytically and synthetically:—

Analytic instruction. "The contemporaneous environment can be analyzed into separate things, the separate things into their component parts, and these last again, into their properties. . . . From presentative instruction (which must be bound up with what the child has hitherto observed) geography and history will gradually develop."[2] "Intercourse can also be analyzed, and we can concentrate the mind on the particular feelings of sympathy which it supplies. . . . A genuine understanding of the feelings of others presupposes the comprehension of one's own. Therefore we must analyze the youthful soul to itself; it should discover in itself the type of the movements of the human mind."[3]

---

[1] *Science of Education*, p. 137. [2] *Ibid.*, p. 174. [3] *Ibid.*, p. 178.

Synthetic in- "Synthetic instruction, which builds with its
struction. own stones, is incomparably richer than the individual environment of the child." Nevertheless Herbart throws out hints[1] as to the manner in which that environment may be utilized in the earliest years, "so that the elements of synthesis, being early made constituent parts of the child's daily experience, may steal imperceptibly into the mind."

Example of in- For explanatory, clear, and suggestive illustra-
struction based tions of the manner in which, on Herbart's prin-
on experience. ciple, experience and intercourse may be used as powerful aids to apperception in every subject of instruction, the reader should consult Herr Lange's work.[2] As examples, especially relating to the extracts from Herbart just given, we take the following:—

First, as to the material of experience in geography and history, "which develop from presentative instruction": "The teacher should see that the pupil may obtain, upon the foundation of numerous observations at home, those indispensable geographical ideas of creek, river, tributary, source and mouth, island, peninsula, and isthmus, plateau and valley, watershed, mountain crest, and pass, etc. He should exercise him diligently in measuring and calculating stretches of road and areas. Thus he will gain in his local home experience, clear and distinct ideas of geographical measurements. These measurements should be closely related to the daily observations of the child—the extent of an acre, a mile or a square mile. He should at all times be able to relate to a neighbouring piece of ground or meadow, a certain section of the road, the division lines of his home district; he should also become acquainted with the different soils of the home district, with its swampy, sandy, and barren tracts, so that he may have at hand definite appropriate images for the marshes, deserts, and plains of geography lessons; he should group and compare what he has by degrees observed concerning the changes of temperature,

---

[1] *Science of Education*, p. 159.
[2] There is an excellent translation of this book by the American Herbart Club, edited by Prof. de Garmo, from which the extracts given in this work are taken.

the position of the sun during the different seasons, the gains
and losses of day and night, the apparent changes of the moon,
and should sketch a map of the celestial bodies with which
he has become familiar. Finally, this study will train the
pupil—and this is not the least of its task—to draw an outline
map not only of his residence town, but also of the entire
home district as far as it is familiar to him, and so to live into
an understanding of the map."[1]

These ideas of valleys, marshes, and forests, the direction
of rivers, the height and position of hills, not as described in
books, but as they actually exist before the child, should be
used to make history living to him. With their help, he should
understand why invading armies landed at certain spots, took
a certain direction, and fought battles where they did, why
settlements were made, and towns were built, and trade flourished in certain localities. For the necessary observations and
concepts of historical instruction, what a wealth of material
London and many other English towns offer! Starting from
the mere names of London streets, with which a London child
is or can be made familiar, a skilful teacher can help him to
people them with the life of the past, and by descriptions,
pictures, and visits to the different spots can bring Roman,
Saxon, Norman, and Elizabethan London in succession before
him. The crowded Walbrook and Fleet Street become once
more the little rivers falling into the Thames, and the three
streams the eastern, western, and southern boundaries and
protections of the first British settlement, a wild moor, now
Moorfields, its northern boundary, and beyond, a vast forest
stretching far away to the northward, the remains of which
are to be seen at Epping. In some such way, a child may get
an idea of the first settlements of our forefathers, and learn
how from barren marsh and dense forest and clay-built huts,
the city of five million people has grown. By a continuous
course of such instruction, much of history may be learned,
as it were, at first hand. It has been well said that geographical and historical instruction which does not thus seek

---

[1] *On Apperception*, Lange, p. 183.

its best help in the home observation of the child, plays on a piano without strings.

Example of instruction based on intercourse. Second, as illustrating what Herbart means by the "analysis of intercourse," take the following:—" The domestic experiences of the child, his intercourse with parents, brothers, sisters, and playmates, his spiritual relation to God—these are the ideas from which the teacher must principally derive the starting-points or aids to apperception. There occurs, for example, in a Bible story the word 'gentle,' and he finds that all do not yet connect with this word a clear idea. Shall he now give a comprehensive definition? No; only from his own experience will it become clear to the pupil what 'gentle' is, as must all else which is to be in reality his own spiritual possession. The teacher reminds the pupil of a night when he suffered with a bad toothache, and his mother took him at last on her lap, and rocking and caressing him, comforted him thus: 'Now it will be better; in the morning it will be all over.' This is a moment when the child forgets the school, but he never forgets the moment. Or if the teacher endeavours to awaken the idea of sympathy, he will accomplish this in the surest manner when he reminds the pupils of experiences of their own, and brings before their minds vividly those occasions in which they rejoiced with the happy and wept with the weeping."[1]

The child's mind must be analyzed to itself. Third, as an application of Herbart's principle that the child's mind must be analyzed to itself, for in it he ought to discover the type of the movements of all human minds, take the following:—" For the understanding of the thought or emotions of historical characters, it is best to direct the child's attention to his own inner experiences, and allow him to linger in thought upon those moments when he was moved with anxiety and dread, or fear and repentance, when the voice of conscience lifted itself to punish, or the satisfaction arising from a kindly and effective deed rejoiced the heart. An occasional quiet return

---

[1] *On Apperception*, Lange.

into one's own inner world, such as history when taught with tact can cause, not only teaches us to understand better what passes in the souls of others, but leads gradually also to right self-knowledge, which is the first condition of self-control."[1]

Instruction must supplement experience and intercourse. Instruction then must know and, as far as possible, use the child's store of experience and intercourse in its own special work, which is *to supplement and extend* these original sources of mental life. For, as Herbart shows, whatever may be their value as aids to the teacher, " the kernel of our mental being cannot be cultivated with certain results by means of experience and intercourse."[2] Firstly, experience is insufficient, because its results, however rich, exist without the teacher's regulative help as "a mass of dispersed and formless fragments," which are powerless to respond with any ordered or sustained thought to the requirements of the mind containing them. Secondly, sympathy is insufficient because "it is not the spirit of intercourse," and therefore the child must learn it elsewhere. " Benevolence and love on one side are not at all sure of arousing similar feelings on the other. The moral reciprocity of intercourse is doubtful, unless kindness is exhibited to the child in such a way as to arouse a similar feeling in his own mind. This can be done by the teacher through his own personality, and through the worthiest characters of humanity supplied by poets and next to them historians."[3] Thirdly, both are insufficient because they do not bring the child into contact with the ideal. It is instruction alone, which shows "that contrast between the actual and what ought to be, which is indispensable to action."[4]

Significance of educative instruction. Under the term "educative instruction" Herbart, as we have seen, understood something essentially different from the usual meaning attached to the word "instruction," which is ordinarily looked upon as a means of imparting knowledge, but only as indirectly exercising an educative influence. In his system, instruction is not only an integral, but the most important part of education. For upon

[1] *On Apperception*, Lange, p. 75.
[2] *Science of Education*, p. 140.   [3] *Ibid.*, p. 139.   [4] *Ibid.*, p. 138.

it devolve the building up of the circle of thought and the welding together, as it were, of the material therein employed, which must be the preparation for any true formation of character—that is, for the formation of will.

Hence Herbart estimates the educative value of instruction solely by the influence it exerts on the will, through the nature of the circle of thought it constructs. In this point he may be compared with Froebel, who writes in the "Education of Man," "The principal aim, the principal point of reference in the guidance of the boy, in the instruction given to him, as well as in the school, is to raise volitional activity to a state of stability and so to vivify and form a clear, vigorous, firm, and enduring will." Not every instruction forms a circle of thought from which a vigorous will proceeds. Even if it imparts knowledge, if it gives a store of clear and animate ideas, they may lie dormant in the mind and hence generate no volition. This is the case when instruction has failed to arouse interest, and has thus missed its end. *Interest* is the keystone of Herbart's conception of instruction, which binds it into a firm and ordered whole. "The final aim of instruction," says Herbart, "is morality. But the nearer aim which instruction in particular must set before itself in order to reach the final one, is *many-sidedness of interest*."[1]

Nature of many-sided interest. What is the nature of this interest which, in Herbart's meaning of the term, it is the aim of instruction to arouse? In answering this question, the essential connection must be borne in mind, which he establishes between interest as the nearer, and formation of character as the final aim of instruction. By this touchstone any kind of interest which does not forward that final aim must be spurious. We shall find in applying it, that interest used as a means of instruction is spurious and must not be appealed to, while interest which is used as the aim of instruction is truly educative.

A teacher sometimes creates an interest in his subject with the object of making the child learn it easily and quickly. The

---

[1] *Umriss pädagogischer Vorlesungen*, 62.

aim of such teaching is *to impress the material*, and several means are used to secure it, among them the arousal of interest.

Again, a teacher sometimes makes the aim of his teaching *the arousal of interest*, and the means he employs thereto, is mental assimilation: apperception.

Receptive and apperceptive interest contrasted. In the first instance the aim leaves the means to be employed undetermined. Any material which will arouse an interest that will secure the object of learning quickly and easily by heart may be used. In the second instance the aim determines the means, for it can be rightly secured in no other way. Both the material and method of instruction are defined. It must be material which is connected with the subject in such a manner, that the ideas given in instruction which are to be apperceived, are brought into connection with ideas already existent in consciousness which can apperceive them, so that mental assimilation—apperception—may take place, for only thus can interest, which is an end in itself, be aroused. Let us consider in an illustration the nature and effect of these two different kinds of interest.

A child is very deficient in power of concentration and inclined to be superficial. Hence her natural tendency is to dislike arithmetic. But she is very fond of music, and has a good ear. In due course she has to learn the multiplication table and cognate rules. This may be done with either of two objects: (1) to commit it to memory as easily and quickly as possible; (2) to learn it in such a way that it will discipline and help to correct her faults of character. According to the object, will be the kind of interest aroused.

If the first be chosen, the mother in teaching this particular child will set the multiplication table, etc., to music. The material that will arouse interest, which is only a means to secure the object, is chosen, and whether that interest has any intrinsic connection with the subject in hand is hence left to chance. In this instance it has not; the interest appealed to is not in numbers, but in music. But the object is secured: the child will learn the multiplication table easily and quickly.

But if the second object be chosen, the mother in teaching this child will arouse her interest in numbers *as* numbers *by means of* numbers. For the interest will now be an end, and apperception[1] a necessary condition to it. Apperception, as we have seen, is the grasping of new ideas by the aid of similar present ones.

True to this principle, the mother, when beginning arithmetic, will remember "the present similar ideas" of the child are concrete, not abstract. She knows the meaning of 2 apples, 3 nuts, but not of 2 and 5; therefore through the former she must be taught to understand the latter. By a number of concrete objects up to 10 apples, etc., she must learn to perceive numbers up to 10 as abstract—symbols which can be used to mark the amounts of any object or objects whatever. By adding these concrete numbers together and then subtracting them in all possible combinations, she will grasp the addition and subtraction of abstract numbers up to 10. At this stage, though she has only this limited knowledge of numbers, she will be capable of understanding the nature of the multiplication table, *i.e.*, that it is nothing more than a convenient way of recording something of what she has already learned—equal additions. She can see that $2+2$ make 4, is precisely the same as 2 taken twice over, or 2 twos make 4, and so on through all the combinations. She will also see that saying, two added to two added to two make six, is the same as saying, three times two are six, but that the first takes much longer than the second, and hence one use of the multiplication table. Having learned that 2 times 2 are 4, she will easily see that if 4 apples are to be arranged in heaps each containing 2, there must be 2 heaps. Having worked this through to 10 apples, the step $4 \div 2 = 2$ is comparatively easy, and hence division by 2 up to 10. The child can now apply the first four rules up to 10 in the solution of little problems, the terms of which are taken from objects she is familiar with. Working on these lines with the guidance of her teacher, she will be able gradually *to make her whole multiplication table for herself.* Any one who has taught arithmetic thus, knows the joyfully active interest which can

---

[1] For nature of apperception see p. 43.

be aroused even in a child naturally disinclined to it, how ready she is to apply what she knows, to set problems to the teacher, and finally to discover rules for herself.

<small>Apperceptive interest influencing formation of character.</small> In this manner the second object is secured. For when once the interest appealed to has been made active by apperception, it will be a powerful agent in correcting the child's faults of character. The absolute truth of numbers can be used to prove to her ocularly, how the slightest inaccuracy on her part produces a wrong result, and *vice versâ* that, given the correctness of her calculations, no other than the one right answer is possible. She is thus through the essence of numbers, as well as through the nature of their processes, encouraged and led to that closeness and continuity of thought, to that habit of steadfast and accurate thinking, which will gradually overcome and replace her superficiality and want of concentration. She will probably take months to learn with the help of the second kind of interest what she would apparently have learned in weeks with the help of the first. Nevertheless it is the first—*receptive interest*—which Herbart rejects whenever possible, because its formative effect is at best very small; it is the second—*apperceptive interest*—which he makes the nearer aim of his instruction, because it must, when once aroused in instruction, make for character.

The knowledge of numbers given by help of the first kind of interest is not, according to Herbart, *educative*. It may remain always more or less dead and worthless; it must do so until later teaching or the child's own experiences fill up the empty concepts. The knowledge received by help of the second kind of interest, directly tends to strengthen the will. For the pleasurable feeling which accompanies knowledge won by apperception again becomes active, when a new demand is made upon the child's mind by instruction. Accompanying the will on the previous occasion, it now directly encourages it to a new effort on behalf both of the apperceiving ideas and those to be apperceived. The will thus aided keeps the new perception, that which is to be apperceived, in consciousness; on the other hand, it chooses from the mind's existing contents and holds fast the apperceiving ideas, those which are related to the new, while it keeps at a distance all not related to it. Thus through interest, instruction forms will.

Herbart's definition of interest. "Interest," then, as Herbart explains, "means in general that species of mental activity which instruction must create, but which has no place in mere knowledge. For we conceive of the latter as a store which the man may entirely dispense with, and yet be no other than with it. He who, on the contrary, holds his knowledge firmly and *seeks to extend it*, is interested in it."[1]

Far-reaching interest. As an illustration of this—the first characteristic of true interest—let us take the following. King Alfred of England, when a child, listened with delight to his mother's reading of an old English poem, and his own wish to read became so strong that the illuminated manuscript containing the poem, being promised to the son who should first learn to do so, was won by him. The interest in literature thus aroused, lived and grew in him amidst all the vicissitudes of his stormy life, so that we are told, "Neither his legislation nor his wars have left such lasting traces on England, as the impulse he gave to its literature."[2] His was a *far-reaching* interest. With mastery of English came the *desire* to learn Latin, and, when in the intervals of peace this seemed possible, the *will* to do it, so that he was able by his translations from the Latin to share his culture with his people, and thus in one sense "created English literature."[3] A far-reaching interest thus is the source of both desire and will. This is the ground on which Herbart claims and maintains for interest its important place in his system of education.

Immediate interest. But interest, besides being far-reaching, must possess three other qualities. It must be *immediate*; that is, it must be its own reward. "Alas," says Goethe, "for that kind of activity which makes us impatient for the end instead of rejoicing by the way!" The activity of true interest must arise from pure, disinterested devotion to the subject in

---

[1] *Science of Education*, p 62. [2] *Short History of the English People*, Green, p. 47. [3] *Ibid.*, p. 48.

hand, not from the desire to gain a creditable school report or a good position in life. For "if any material charm seizes the boy strongly, he will calculate, and then he is lost to pure morality."[1] The teacher therefore must carefully avoid in instruction everything which furthers the growth of mediate, and hinders the rise of immediate interest. The ground for doing so leads us directly to the third essential quality of interest.

Many-sided Interest. "Mediate interest," says Herbart, "tends, the greater its extent to one-sidedness, if not to egoism. The egoist is interested in a thing only to the extent to which it is advantageous or disadvantageous to him. The one-sided man is akin to the egoist, even if so unconsciously, for he connects everything with the narrow circle in which he lives and thinks."

If literature had formed practically the whole of King Alfred's circle of thought, if his interest had been *only* farreaching, the work demanded from him by his age as warrior and statesman would have been left undone. He would have been a one-sided man. To avoid the danger of egoism, and to provide that breadth of culture which will enable a man to command circumstances in the way which may seem to him morally best, interest must be *many-sided*.

"Interest," says Herbart, "arises from interesting objects; many-sided interest originates in the wealth of these, and to create and develop it is the task of instruction."[2] In the process, the child's individuality is to be left as untouched as possible. "The projections, the strength of individuality, may remain so far as they do not spoil the character; through them the entire outline may take this or that form."[3] On the other hand, individuality must to some extent be changed by widened interest, it must approximate to a general form, "or it will not be amenable to the general obligatory moral law."[4] The teacher must duly weigh and take into account both these claims of individuality and many-sidedness, for "the more in-

---

[1] *Æsthetic Revelation of the World*, p. 68.
[2] *Science of Education*, p. 120. [3] *Ibid.*, p. 120. [4] *Ibid.*, p. 121.

dividuality is blended with many-sidedness, the more easily will the character assert its sway over the individual."[1]

" In the many-sidedness of interest, the child will find protection in the future against the yoke of the desires and passions. It will arm him against fortune's changes, and will make life worth living, even when a cruel fate has robbed him of his dearest. It will guard him from all errors which spring from idleness, and will provide him with a new calling when the old has been closed to him. It will raise him to the level from which earthly possessions and the success of worldly efforts seem but accidents, which cannot touch the true self, for above them stands the moral character grand and free."[2] On the ground of its importance as a factor in education, Herbart made the quality of many-sidedness the basis of his following division of interest.

Divisions of many-sided interest. Many-sided interest he divides into interest arising from knowledge, and interest arising from sympathy.

Interest arising from knowledge is of three kinds:—

Empirical interest. First, empirical interest, which grows from knowledge gained by experience and observation of manifold phenomena. This knowledge excites pleasure in the mind by the strength, change, and novelty of the impressions produced; and the desire to progress in it is the result of an empirical interest.

Speculative interest. Second, speculative interest, aroused by the consciousness of the mysterious and the obscure, excites a desire to pass from mere empirical observation to the investigation of the origin of, and causal relations between phenomena.

Æsthetic interest. Third, æsthetic interest is aroused neither by phenomena nor their causes, but by " the approval which their harmony and adaptability to an end win from us."[3] It is synonymous with interest in the naturally, artistically, or morally beautiful.

---

[1] The reader will find an account of the manner in which Herbart reconciles many-sided interest and individuality in *Science of Education*, Translator's Introduction, p. 34.
[2] *Grundriss der Pädagogik*, Kern 12.   [3] *Kleine Schriften*, Herbart.

Illustrations of interest arising from knowledge. These three classes of interest arising from knowledge may be illustrated from biology. The various characteristics of individual animals would appeal to *empirical interest*; the theory of evolution of species by natural selection would appeal to *speculative interest*; the adaptation of animals to their circumstances and mode of life (*e.g.*, protective colouring) would appeal to *æsthetic interest*.

Sympathetic interest. Interest arising from sympathy is also of three kinds. First, sympathetic interest is personal, and springs from intercourse. It is aroused by the reproduction in the individual of the feelings of others in their varieties of joy and sorrow, pleasure and pain.

Social interest. Second, social interest. When to the former feeling are added a comprehension of the larger relationships of society, and a participation in that which makes the weal or woe of the many, that general interest in the progress of humanity arises which Herbart calls social interest.

Religious interest. Third, religious interest is developed, when this enlarged sympathy is directed to the history and destiny of the entire human race. When understanding and feeling become clear, that the guidance of humanity and the direction of the individual lot are alike withdrawn from human power, then the heart is filled with fear and hope. " Belief springs out of need," [1] and religious interest is awakened.

Illustrations of interest arising from sympathy. These three classes of interest arising from sympathy may be illustrated from literature—George Eliot's " Romola." Her protest to Tito against the sale of her father's library as a breach of trust, would appeal to *sympathetic interest*. " You talk of substantial good, Tito! Are faithfulness, and love, and sweet, grateful memories no good? Is it no good we should keep our silent promises, on which others build because they believed in our love and truth? Is it no good that a just life should be justly honoured? . . . I am thinking of my father, and of my love and sorrow for him, and of his just claims on us. It was a yearning of *his* heart,

---

[1] *Science of Education*, p. 135.

and therefore it is a yearning of mine." Savonarola's prayer to her to use her sorrow as the road to a wider sympathy, and to return to the suffering people of Florence, would appeal to *social interest*. "Your dead wisdom has left you without a heart for the neighbours among whom you dwell; it has left you without a share in the Divine life which quenches the sense of suffering self in the ardours of an ever-growing love. You think nothing of the sorrow and the wrong that are within the walls of the city where you dwell; you would leave your place empty, when it ought to be filled with your pity and your labour. If there is wickedness in the streets, your steps should shine with the light of purity; if there is a cry of anguish, you my daughter, because you know the meaning of the cry, should be there to still it." Lastly, Romola's repudiation of the limits Savonarola sets to the all-embracing love of God, would appeal to *religious interest*. "Take care, father," said Romola, "lest your enemies have some reason, when they say that in your visions of what will further God's kingdom, you see only what will strengthen your own party." "And that is true!" said Savonarola, with flashing eyes. "The cause of my party *is* the cause of God's kingdom." "I do not believe it," said Romola, her whole frame shaken with passionate repugnance. "God's kingdom is something wider, else let me stand outside it with the beings that I love."

An illustration of the six classes of interest. In the cultivation of these six classes of interest, many-sidedness is secured. How would they be appealed to by an event in English history—for instance, the defeat of the Spanish Armada? The contrast between the little fleet of England, supplied to a great extent by the devotion of her people, and the immense armament of Spain; the characteristic pluck and daring of the conquering Englishmen—Hawkins, who had been the first to break into the charmed circle of the Indies, Frobisher, the hero of the Northwest Passage, and Drake, who commanded the privateers—their devotion to their country and queen, as typical of the whole navy; the events of the encounter; a comparison between the build of the Spanish and English ships, and the superiority of the latter; the defeat of the so-called Invincible

Armada by Englishmen—all this is calculated to arouse *empirical interest.*

Inquiry into the cause of the enmity between England and Spain, and an attempt to measure the actual effect on Europe of the victory of England contrasted with the probable results had the Spaniards been victorious—this would arouse *speculative interest.*

The Queen's courage, the wisdom and self-abnegation of her councillors, the bravery and enterprise of her soldiers and sailors, the loyalty and enthusiasm of her people, as described, for instance, by Kingsley in *Westward Ho, all working together for the end* of England's freedom, would appeal to *æsthetic interest.*

Again, the Queen placed in so difficult and dangerous a position, and yet so courageous, England's forces commanded by her in person, and her dauntless determination, declared in her address to them, to live and die if need be, with her people [1]; her prayer to the Lord of battles; her thought of the fire-ships, and her command to Drake to send them into the midst of the Armada; the ensuing panic, and the medal struck in its commemoration, with a device of fire-ships scattering the Spanish fleet, and the words, "Dux fœmina facti"—"It was done by a woman"—all this would appeal to, and arouse *sympathetic interest.*

We are told by a Roman Catholic writer, whose testimony in favour of Protestant England we may presumably trust, that when the land was threatened by the Spanish invasion "all party feelings, all sectarian divisions and jealousies, were laid aside, for every bosom appeared overflowing with that generous and ennobling principle of exalted patriotism, which Burke has truly called 'the cheap defence of nations.'" [2] *Social interest*

---

[1] "I am come among you at this time resolved, in the midst of the heat of battle, to live and die amongst you all. Rather than any dishonour should grow by me, I myself will take up arms; I myself will be your general, judge, and rewarder of every one of your virtues in the field; and I doubt not but by your obedience to my general, by your concord in the camp, and your valour in the field, we shall shortly have a famous victory over these enemies of my God, of my kingdoms, and of my people" (*Life of Queen Elizabeth*, Mademoiselle Keralio).

[2] *Lives of the Queens of England*, Agnes Strickland.

would be aroused in the reader by this passionate enthusiasm, which beat as one pulse in the English nation.

After the defeat of the Armada, Elizabeth and her people went in joyful procession to St. Paul's to return thanks for England's victory. In the cathedral, hung with banners and other trophies taken from the Spaniards, the Queen, surrounded by her councillors and subjects, knelt in silent prayer, then heard the chanting of the Litany and the sermon from the Bishop of Salisbury on the words, "He blew with His winds, and they were scattered." "The great sea-fight had determined whether Popery and despotism, or Protestantism and freedom were the law which God had appointed for the half of Europe and the whole of future America."[1] This general national thanksgiving which followed it—ruler and people made one by a common danger and a common rescue, and perceiving through both "the traces of Providence in the slow, solemn, often apparently retrogressive, but yet ever-advancing progress of the world"[2]—all this would appeal to and arouse *religious interest*.

Balanced interest. To avoid one-sidedness, interest must not only be many-sided; unless the six classes of interest be *equally* cultivated, one-sidedness amidst many-sidedness may still take place. Herbart illustrates the manner in which this may be guarded against thus: "We find, for instance, that the pupil is more inclined from his environment to social, possibly to patriotic, interests than to sympathy with individuals, or that he is prompted to value matters of taste more than those of speculation, or *vice versâ*; in each case the fault is equally great. First, the mass on the side of the overweight must be analyzed, completed, arranged; secondly, the balance must be restored, partly in connection with this, partly directly through instruction." The teacher must *never* encourage one-sidedness. "By no means should the presence of incidental prominent tendencies in the years of cultivation be regarded as a sign, that they are to be further strengthened by education."[3] In Herbart's words,

---

[1] *Westward Ho!* Charles Kingsley. [2] Herbart's fourth letter to Herr von Steiger. [3] *Science of Education*, p. 142.

"many-sided, far-reaching, immediate interest must be also harmonious, proportioned, *balanced*."

Interest the motive power in education. Herbart may be said to be the first who assigned to interest its true place as the *greatest motive power in education*. Many before him had indicated, and even tried to estimate, the force that interest might become under the guidance of a genuine teacher, but his was the first attempt to formulate a complete theory of interest. Quintilian, 1,700 years before Herbart had written, "Studium discendi voluntate quæ cogi non potest constat"; and Rollin, gathering up the testimony of this and a host of other witnesses, expressed the same truth 1,600 years later thus: "We should never lose sight of the grand principle that *study depends on the will*, and the will does not endure constraint." Herbart, in his theory of instruction and in his practical work as teacher, recognized the truth of this principle, and took it as his guide. Many, however, among both his predecessors and successors have done so also; therefore it cannot be the principle which marks him out as the originator of a new departure in education. For that which is distinctive of him we must look *within* the principle—to the answer he gave to the question it raises; since study depends on the will, *how* is the will to be reached? By the power of apperceptive interest, he replies. Through apperceptive interest Herbart, as we have seen, appeals directly to the will, and draws it without constraint, by the gentle attraction of assimilated knowledge, into the service of instruction. It is this, his interpretation of the principle, which may without exaggeration be called a great discovery, one which, as it becomes more widely known and understood, will tend to mould all true education in the future. Others have attempted, and still attempt, to stimulate the activity of the will by external deterrents and inducements: self-interest, emulation, fear of punishment, hope of reward, and love of praise. It remained for Herbart not only to recognize interest as the true psychologic instrument by which the work of education ought to be done, but to demonstrate in his analysis of it, the nature and efficacy of its operations when guided by a true teacher. As the *natural* force for the work of education, it carries with it no corresponding evil, while by the use of other means, serious moral harm may and to some degree must be done to the pupil. Herbart, it is true, recognizes the love of approbation (not of praise) as a motive rightly active in the young ; but, since it is appealed to directly by discipline and only indirectly by instruction, any reference to it will come under the former division of education.

"Interest," says Dr. R. Staude, "is the light with which Herbart has once for all illumined with the brightness of day the dark and mysterious ways of the art of teaching ; it is the magic word which alone gives instruction the power to call out the minds of the young and make them serve the master's aims; it is the long lever of education which, moved easily and gladly by the teacher, can alone bring the will of the young into the desired direction and activity."

How is interest created? How then, is interest created ? An exhaustive answer to this question is here impossible, and we must be content with a few indications. We have seen that when the union of new with older presentations takes place easily and surely, a feeling of satisfaction arises, which again produces a desire for a repetition of the inner activity, and a need for further occupation with the same object. "To the pleasurable feeling is easily added the effort, at a favourable opportunity to reproduce the product of the apperception, to supplement and deepen it, to unite it to other ideas, and so further to extend certain chains of thought. The summit or the sum of these states of mind we happily express by the word *interest*. For in reality, the feeling of self appears between the various stages of the process of apperception (*inter esse*); with one's whole soul does one contemplate the object of attention. If we regard the acquired knowledge as the *objective* side of apperception, interest must be regarded as its *subjective* side."[1] Interest, then, is essentially connected with apperception. To arouse interest two conditions are necessary : first, that the new shall find masses of apperceiving presentations existent in the mind, and second, that the process of apperception, the fusion of the new with the old, shall take place with ease and satisfy an inner need.

---

[1] *On Apperception*, Lange, p. 19.

To ensure these conditions, (1) the *treatment* of the material of instruction must be determined by psychological principles; that is, the teacher's method must be based on the psychical process in the mind of the child : (2) the *selection* of the material of instruction must be determined by the child's capacity for comprehending it; that is, it must be suited to the particular stage of apperception he has arrived at. The treatment of the material of instruction is founded on the theory of the *formal steps*; the selection of the material is determined by the theories of the *concentration centres* and the *culture epochs*. The theory of the formal steps is undoubtedly Herbart's; the theories of the concentration centres and the culture epochs are, as will be seen, developments of his school, about which there is much diversity of opinion. They will now be considered in the next section in order.

PROF. REIN'S CLASSIFICATION OF EDUCATIVE INSTRUCTION.
TWO SPHERES OF MATERIAL.

A.—LIFE OF MAN. Historical-Humanistic Branches.				B.—LIFE OF NATURE. Branches of Natural Science.		
I. INSTRUCTION FOR TRAINING THE DISPOSITION.	II. ART INSTRUCTION.			III. LANGUAGE INSTRUCTION.	I. GEOGRAPHY.	II. NATURAL SCIENCE.	III. MATHEMATICS (ARITHMETIC).
	Drawing.	Modelling.	Singing.	Mother-tongue.	Foreign Languages.			
Biblical and Ecclesiastical History.	Profane History.	Literature.				Other material for culture epoch 6 as above given in detail, p. 145.
Concentration material for culture epoch 6. Age 11—12 years.				Other material for culture epoch 6 as above given in detail, p. 145.		
Life of Jesus.	Voyages of Discovery.	Life of Wiclif.				

CHAPTER III. (*continued*)

PRACTICAL PEDAGOGY

SECTION II.—TREATMENT OF THE MATERIAL OF INSTRUCTION;
THEORY OF THE FORMAL STEPS

Classification of the material of instruction. The material of instruction is contained, says Herbart, in the sciences. But the names of the sciences are not sufficient for the classification of the material. The cognate materials in the different branches must be brought out, and these Herbart classifies as symbols, forms, and things. Symbols—for instance languages—are only interesting as the media of description. In themselves they are wearisome, and therefore, he emphatically says, should be used at first only so far as they can be applied to the description of what interests.[1] Forms also, the single properties of things, selected and considered individually, are not immediately interesting, and therefore, must "always be kept in close contact with actuality"[2]—with the objects which supply them. Finally, things, works of nature and of art, arouse immediate interest. Since they are nothing else than "complications or complexions"[3] of properties taken out by abstraction, and considered separately, we can proceed either from these single properties to the things in which they are combined, or from the things themselves, separating them into their properties.

Accordingly the course of instruction is determined as analytic or synthetic. It is analytic when it is broken up and articulated, and at the same time corrected and completed; it is synthetic when the elements are given, and afterwards combined.

Theory of the formal steps. The treatment of the material—*i.e.*, the method—of instruction, is considered by Herbart in his chap-

---

[1] *Science of Education*, p. 150.   [2] *Ibid.*, p. 150.   [3] *Ibid.*, p. 29.

ters entitled "Steps and Course of Instruction." The abstract conceptions therein contained have been reduced by Prof. Ziller, of Leipsic, to the theory of the formal steps, and still further simplified by Prof. Rein, of Jena, whose classification we shall here adopt and translate. These steps are founded on strictly psychologic principles. They are simply the division and development of every lesson the child receives, according to the psychical process which takes place in his mind.

Method units. The material of instruction for a given time must in the first instance be divided into small sections or *method units*, in Herbart's words, "a little group of objects."[1] These units must not be too large, or their retention will be difficult, nor too small, or the material will be insufficient. They must each contain one clear, general truth, which it is the *aim* of the lesson or series of lessons to exhibit. For it by no means follows that a method unit can be worked through in an hour's lesson. While that time is often sufficient for an arithmetic, a geometry, or a natural science unit, one of history, language, or geography will sometimes require several hours. When the method unit thus extends over several lessons, a subordinate or hour aim for each lesson must be set up. The teacher must, as a rule, supply the aim for the method unit. When subordinate aims are required—that is, when the method unit extends beyond an hour's lesson—the children can generally supply them, and should always be encouraged to do so.

The aim of the method unit. This statement of the aim is to be made at the *beginning* of every lesson. It must be a question, or exercise, or fact of experience, having a concrete content. "It must never be permitted to take the form of a general idea or general opinion, for it is clear that the abstract cannot be given, that, on the contrary, it is to be gradually developed from a group of similar ideas."[2] And it must be related to the child's already existent store of ideas. These conditions being present, the statement of the aim has the following advantages:—(1) The teacher knows exactly what presentations he requires as apper-

---

[1] *Science of Education*, p. 151.   [2] *On Apperception*, Lange, p. 206.

ceiving helps, and thus "is prevented and protected in advance from a vague roaming round in the field of the pupil's experiences." (2) The pupil is placed in a state of expectation, the most favourable condition of mind for the growth of interest. (3) The definite aim directly promotes apperception, for it encourages and helps the pupil to raise related ideas into consciousness, and thus develops independent mental activity. (4) It is a powerful incentive to willing. "The pupil must know from the beginning what is the matter at issue, if he is to use all his energy in learning, and he will so use it if he knows exactly what is to be attained. *Without aim, no will.*" [1]

The five steps according to Rein and Herbart. The statement of the aim introduces the five formal steps. They are so called because all material of instruction, however various its contents, must be worked through in the *form* these steps prescribe. We give Rein's classification and Herbart's parallel terminology, which will be found in the *Science of Education*. [2]

THE FIVE FORMAL STEPS.

Rein.	Herbart and Ziller.
Preparation (*Vorbereitung*)	Analysis.
Presentation (*Darbietung*)	Synthesis.
Association (*Verknüpfung*)	Association.
Recapitulation (*Zusammenfassung*)	System.
Application (*Anwendung*)	Method.

Analysis as used by Herbart and Ziller means nothing more than the analysis of the ideas already existent in the child's mind, which are related to the new material; synthesis is the apperception of the new by the old. Together they produce what Herbart calls clearness of the particulars. Recapitulation is called by Herbart system, and application is method. The term "method" used in this connection by him must not be confused with that wider use of it in the expression "method of teaching," where it covers the whole of the formal steps. Herbart prescribes the use of the formal steps in these words:

---

[1] *Das erste Schuljahr*, Rein, Pickel, u. Scheller.
[2] *Science of Education*, p. 126.

"In every group of its objects" (*i.e.*, in every method unit), "instruction must care equally and in regular succession for clearness of every particular" (analysis and synthesis, or preparation and presentation), "for association of the manifold" (association), "for coherent ordering of what is associated" (recapitulation), "and for a certain practice in progression through this order" (application).[1]

In working through the five steps of a method unit, the pupil passes through two psychical processes, *i.e.*, firstly, *apperception*, which is completed when, by the first two steps—analysis, or preparation of the old, and synthesis, or presentation of the new—the old and new have been fused together; secondly, *abstraction*, which is completed when, by the third step similar objects are compared and combined, and by the fourth step any general truths they contain are elicited. The fifth and final step directs the application of the acquired knowledge. The result of the two processes has been defined as the growth and condensation of concepts from percepts.

First formal step: preparation.—In the preceding chapter on psychology we have seen (1) that if presentations are to become an integral part of the mind, they must be apperceived; (2) that this process can only take place between similar or related presentations. If then the new is to be assimilated by the pupil, we must ask, *What presentations are there in his mind which are related to the new?* Before the new ones are offered to him, these old presentations—the apperceiving ones—must be brought up *clearly* into consciousness. To secure this the teacher must make sure (1) that they are sufficiently numerous, (2) sufficiently clear, (3) and are in the right order to apperceive the new. Generally they are not so, and the teacher must arouse some, complete and make others clear, and arrange all in the order in which they will be required. As the farmer ploughs the soil before casting in the seed, so also must the teacher carefully dig over the mental field, before sowing in it the seed of new knowledge. To bring the mind into such a condition that the germs to be given in

---

[1] *Science of Education*, p. 144.

the lesson will become fruitful, is the work of preparation.
Thus its character is at once determined: its function is not to
offer anything new, but to analyze the child's circle of thought,
and to cut out from it that part which will be required, rejecting the rest as indifferent. Preparation may be divided into
two parts, the first of which the teacher undertakes alone, the
second with his pupils. First, before every lesson the teacher
must ask himself, What *do* my pupils know of the subject in
hand? and, What *ought* they to know if they are to understand
it thoroughly? Every teacher ought to be sufficiently acquainted with his pupils, to fairly estimate the extent of the
knowledge he can assume in them. This ought to determine
the range and contents of the new. If he puts no such questions to himself, he will assume too much, or choose a subject
too difficult or too remote, or he will not make it sufficiently
clear and intelligible. He must know what apperceiving ideas
his pupils have, if he is to fill up the more or less empty ones,
and arrange all in the order most advantageous to the grasp of
the new. Second, after the aim has been stated, the teacher
asks his pupils, " What do you already know about the subject
of our lesson? Tell me everything you can think of about it."
First one scholar answers; then the others improve and complete
his answer. This they must be encouraged to do in their own
natural unfettered way, even if their style be faulty, and the
arrangement of their knowledge unsystematic. " We must allow
the pupil to express himself in a free, unrestrained manner
about the subjects of his experience, not avoiding even the most
peculiarly related events, in order that a complete absorption in
familiar ideas, those strongest aids to apperception, may precede
the presentation of the related new ideas." Then, to make good
the pupils' faults and omissions in these narrations, the whole
is combined, arranged, and recapitulated. "The apperceiving
ideas must frequently be collected and arranged. If we passed
the material but once, and in the order in which it would
occur by chance, many contradictions would remain unrecon-
ciled, and many principal thoughts not seldom be lost in a mass
of incidentals. A brief summing up, suitable to the contents of
the ideas, and a separation of the essential from the unessential,

is therefore absolutely necessary, and not less so, sufficient repetition and impressing of that which as yet shows itself uncertain and wavering." All that relates to the new is thus brought clearly into consciousness; it is ready to apperceive the new, and the preparation is completed. The more advanced the pupil, the better can he make this analytical preparation for himself without the teacher's aid.

Many teachers use preparation incorrectly, firstly so when they make it an address, and introduce into it new presentations which belong to the next stage. Then the degree of mental activity and interest, which is necessary to make instruction successful, is not reached.

"From first to last that form of preparation in which the teacher alone takes part, which subjects the pupil to discourses by him, and which the pupil must silently follow, must be declared inadmissible." When the child is allowed an opportunity of expressing his own vivid experiences, the most frozen-up mind thaws, the lesson appears interesting, and the teacher gains in the preparation a wellspring of expectant attention.

Secondly, it is an error to introduce the known material into the next stage (presentation). The child is then expected to do two things at the same time: to remember the old and to unite the new with it; thereby both processes are curtailed. The old material is not strong enough to grasp the new perfectly, and the new sinks below the threshold of consciousness.

Thirdly, it is a yet worse error to call up the known presentations *after* the new. It is putting the cart before the horse, for the new, which found no points of adhesion, has already partially vanished, and the after-calling to mind of the known ideas is merely an attempt to make good a mistake which ought never to have been made.

The next stage—the presentation of the new—is not successful unless the preparation has been rightly made, and a mental appetite created, so that the old presentations stand, as it were, ready to spring up, seize, and master the new.[1]

---

[1] The student by frequently referring to a model lesson on the honey-bee, given at the end of this analysis of the formal steps, will easily follow their development.

Second formal step: presentation.—"It consists in either relating a story (to little children), reading a selection on an historical topic (to riper pupils), or in showing and carefully observing a natural object or a geometrical body, an exercise in arithmetic for the solution of a problem, a geographical subject exhibited upon the board or sought upon a map and described, an incident in natural science brought up and investigated." Presentation is mainly governed (1) by the law of successive clearness, and (2) by the law of the alternation of concentration and reflection.[1]

The law of successive clearness. The law of successive clearness produces, in one word, order. A collection of books piled one on the other in confusion is, on account of the time spent in searching for what is wanted, practically useless for reference purposes. In a well-ordered library, on the contrary, any book needed can be found almost in the dark. Just so ought the pupil to be able to find and grasp rapidly, instinctively, and without reflection, the presentations which the mind contains as they are required. Teaching produces such clearness in the mind when the presentations it supplies and uses are not heaped up anyhow, but are given in single, small sections. The parts and their sequence are determined, not by the teacher's caprice, but by the nature of the subject in hand. In the insect, for example, we consider—(1) the head; (2) the thorax; (3) the posterior part of the body; (4) the appendages of the body; in an historical subject—(1) its actual contents, time, place, persons, action; (2) its psychological course of development; (3) its moral aspects. When the teaching is thus ordered, the pupil clearly comprehends the individual parts.

The law of the alternation of concentration and reflection. The law of the alternation of concentration and reflection provides, not only that the pupil shall know the individual parts, but shall grasp their connection and combination into a whole. Let us suppose the subject of the lesson is divided into four parts. The teacher takes, to begin with, the first—the head of the bee, for example. Attention is fixed on that alone; there is no reference whatever

---

[1] *Science of Education*, pp. 126 and 144.

to the remaining three parts. The pupil *concentrates* himself on it; each property and peculiarity is exhibited or elicited, so that it is thoroughly examined and known. Every part is thus treated successively, till all are known *as* parts. These psychical acts are called by Herbart concentrations. The function of concentration is to see single things distinctly. This can only be if, according to the law of successive clearness already noticed, " the several varied concentrations disintegrated by the teacher's care are presented one by one." [1]

But the pupil must not only know the parts of a lesson *as* parts: he must also know them in their connection with each other, that is, as a whole. In Herbart's words, " reflection must follow concentration." "Concentration puts the parts into the pupils' hands, but the mental links are missing." *To restore these mental links between the just separated parts* is the work of reflection. It consists in a *connecting* recapitulation of the parts, following the preliminary division of the whole into them. Since it by no means follows that knowledge of the parts necessitates knowledge also of their intrinsic connection, reflection is a most important act in presentation. The pupil must be able to repeat the whole in any and every variety of sequence; not till then will he grasp its connection as well as the contents of its parts. The passage from part to part allows " those necessary pauses to be made which give opportunity for a review of the ground covered, and a moment of reflection to follow regularly a state of concentration on the subject. Let short, topical statements and key-words be placed on the blackboard, which indicate the particular points on which attention must be fixed, and which assist in retaining the idea. Finally, the separate parts, each of which has been made prominent for the sake of clearness, must be united and combined into a unity in consciousness." [2]

Mental respiration. "It is a universal requirement," says Herbart, " that concentration and reflection should alternate with each other; together they constitute mental respiration.[3]

---

[1] *Science of Education*, p. 126.   [2] *On Apperception*, Lange, p. 214.
[3] *Lehrbuch zur Psychologie*, p. 213.

Concentration, above all, must precede reflection; both must be kept as near as possible together. Instruction must follow the rule of giving equal weight, in every smallest possible group of its objects, to concentration and reflection.[1] It is the possession of a rich reflection, and the completest power of reverting at will into every concentration, which makes a man many-sided."[2] Presentation closes with a recapitulation of the whole by a pupil, not in the form of answers to the teacher's questions, but as a connected reproduction by himself. Then his faults are corrected, and his omissions supplied by the rest of the class.

As before observed, with the two steps of preparation and presentation, the first psychical process—viz., apperception—is completed. Both preparation and presentation—analysis and synthesis—must be perfect, otherwise the following steps are impossible. "There can be no system, no order, no relationship, without clearness in single things."[3] The third step is the first of the second psychical process: abstraction.

Third formal step: association. *Third formal step: association.*—The pupil, having passed the two steps just considered, clearly knows *a single object*: the honey-bee; a geometrical principle; a poem; an event in history. With this, however, the aim of teaching is but half reached; only empirical, not speculative interest is satisfied by the knowledge of particulars. What is learned is, to begin with, an isolated fact or object, from which, however, the mind must learn to rise to the general, to those universal and necessary laws which in the transitions of phenomena remain always unchanged—for example, to the *rules* of grammar, the *laws* which govern the psychical and material world, the *maxims* of morality, the *principles* of art, in short, to concepts and causes. The uncultured mind is limited by single things and externals; the cultured rises to concepts, and pierces to causes. The teacher must start the pupil on this road; hence he must never be satisfied with his comprehension, however clear, of single things, but must stimulate him to find the universal rule, the law, the cause, which governs a group of single things. These universals he

---

[1] *Science of Education*, p. 144.   [2] *Ibid.*, p. 124.   [3] *Ibid.*, p. 127.

must, as far as possible, discover himself, and do so in the third step: association. It regulates in three ways the formation of general concepts: (1) by comparison of things similar and related ; (2) by comparison of contrasts ; (3) by changes of sequence.

1. By comparison of things similar and related. The pupil, for example, has learned in previous lessons about the Alps, the Caucasus, the Himalayas, and the Cordilleras. In this third step we ask him what, notwithstanding their differences of situation, all these mountain ranges have in common. All rise above the range of vegetation; all are covered with eternal snow and glaciers; all are *high ranges*, being above 2,600 metres; and are distinguished by these characteristics from the *medium* ranges, which do not possess them. Thus the pupil forms the concept of high range, and can also deduce the conclusion from it that Kilmandscharo, which is above 6,000 metres high, must have the characteristics of a high mountain, and thus must be covered with snow and glaciers, although beneath the tropical sun of Africa.

2. By comparison of contrasts. For instance, the pupil has learned in the geography of England about the Northern, the Cambrian, and the Devonian ranges, and besides the European Alps. If he now compares the Cambrian range with the Alps, a number of differences appear which contain the characteristics of medium and high ranges, and thus from the comparison of contrasts both these concepts are formed.

3. By variations of sequence. A child learns to count 1, 2, 3, 10, 100, and if allowed only to do so thus, will imagine there is no other way. But he can work backwards—100, 99, etc.—and again with 8, 16, 24, in short, in every variety of numerical sequence. Arithmetic is really nothing more than the working through of numerical series in every possible direction. But it is governed by fixed laws, and to make these clear to the pupil (in addition, subtraction, multiplication, and division) is the object of teaching arithmetic. Through the constantly varying series of numbers, the general concepts they contain (arithmetical rules) must be elicited. For instance, a child has six marbles, his schoolfellow nine. The latter has three more than the former ($9-6=3$). If I give two more to

each, the difference remains the same (11−8=3). From such examples a pupil will conclude a general truth: that if it be desirable to add equal sums to numbers whose difference we want to find, the accuracy of the answer will not be affected.

Fourth formal step: recapitulation. Fourth formal step: recapitulation (for generalization and classification).—The course of teaching so far, has given the pupil the subject matter from which concepts have been formed. But these concepts must not be left in a state of confusion in his mind. The fourth step must gradually arrange the acquired concepts in the series and groups which their nature necessitates, so that the pupil may gradually see them as an ordered whole. This systematic order is again the parallel to the well-arranged library, in which a book can be instantly found. Upon it depend the readiness of thought, the power to reach and apply a rule readily and without hesitation. Hence this theoretical arrangement is the necessary preliminary to all practical application. It is, as it were, the vast mountain lake into which flow all the mountain springs and rivers, which are afterwards to be turned to the practical use of the towns beneath. As an example, we may take the system of grammar. A pupil translates a methodically arranged French, or Latin, or German piece. In doing so he learns the various forms of speech, the different cases of the declinations, the tenses of the conjugations, the use of prepositions and conjunctions, for example, that when the meaning is "so that," "in order that," *ut* is employed in Latin with the conjunctive, but when the meaning is "when," "as," *cum* is used. Gradually everything which is connected is arranged together until the pupil ultimately sees in Latin the five declensions, the comparisons, the pronouns, the numerals, the regular and irregular conjugations, the syntax; in short, when he leaves school, he has a clear knowledge of the whole structure of the language.

It is obvious that younger pupils cannot go far beyond the process of apperception. Their perceptions are neither sufficiently numerous nor complete, to be the basis of generalization; therefore the process of abstraction as a whole is impossible to them. In their case, "the material of instruction ends with the acquisition of series and groups of ideas, as, for example, of the traits of an historical person, a series of dates, a group of grammatical forms, the description of a country, the drawing of mountains and river valleys; and it must be reserved for later consideration to unite these results with others into a higher form of knowledge."[1] "The complete carrying out of the formal steps from the lowest to the highest class is only justified, when the notion of system is changed according to the need, that is, when we understand by the word at one time general notions and what is universally valid, at another only dispositions and material for the making of general notions." Herbart warns against a premature attempt to stimulate generalizing, and points out the sufficiency, if well worked through, of the two first steps—*i.e.*, the process of apperception—for young pupils thus: "The union of the groups presupposes the perfect unity of each group. So long, therefore, as it is still possible for the last particular in the content of each group to fall apart from the rest, higher reflection cannot be thought of. We must be contented in earlier years with not attempting to give what we call system in the higher sense, but must, on the other hand, so much the more create clearness in every group; we must associate the groups the more sedulously and variously, and be careful that the approach to the all-embracing reflection is made equally from all sides." Herbart defines system as "the perfect order of a copious reflection."[2]

Fifth formal step: application. Fifth formal step: application.—A multitude of concepts, even if systematically arranged, is of little use to a mind which cannot use them as required by the needs of daily life. How to utilize practically the acquired concepts, rules, laws, etc., then, is the necessary and final step of teaching, viz., application. It may be taught in a variety of ways. "The series of ideas or concepts may be repeated forward or backward from different starting-points, and under different circumstances. The child may be required to pass from the concept to the individual perceptions

---

[1] *On Apperception*, Lange, p. 234.   [2] *Science of Education*, p. 127.

(deduction), and *vice versâ* (induction). In the case of historical instruction, examples may be gathered from history or the child's life, which either conform or do not conform to a given maxim. In the various branches of language instruction, examples may be sought that conform to some grammatical rule, and conversely the pupil may determine which rule governs a given form, etc. Written and spoken exercises conform to the grammatical system which he has thus far attained. In mathematics and the natural sciences, the geometric, arithmetical, and physical formulas and laws may be applied in solving practical problems and tasks, or a physical apparatus may be drawn to conform to certain given conditions. In geography a general map may be sketched from memory, or commercial, physical, and political facts applied in imaginary cases."[1]

It is this continuous application of newly acquired knowledge to previously existent groups of ideas, and the power which grows from it of passing through these groups at will, which constitutes what Herbart terms an *interconnected* circle of thought. The characteristics which a circle of thought ought to possess, whose store of presentations has been acquired and ordered through the formal steps of instruction, are thus given by him: " In it everything must circulate easily and freely; everything must be in its place, ready to be found and used at any moment; nothing must lie in the way, and nothing, like a heavy load, impede useful activity. Clearness, association, system, and method must rule there." As the direct support of courage, without which volition is paralyzed, the effect of such a circle of thought on character is very great. "Courage, then, will be sustained by the certainty of the *inner* performance, and rightly so, for the external impediments which unexpectedly appear to the foresight of a careful intelligence can terrify him but little who knows that, with altered circumstances, he can at once evolve new plans."[2]

There are thus five formal steps which must be taken in the treatment of a method unit, though not necessarily in an hour's lesson, for as a rule a method unit requires for its treat-

---
[1] *Outlines of Pedagogics*, Prof. Rein, translated by C. and T. van Liew.
[2] *Science of Education*, p. 213.

ment more than one lesson. They are preparation, or *Vorbereitung* (in Herbart's terminology, analysis); presentation, or *Darstellung* (synthesis); association, or *Verknüpfung*[1] (*association*); recapitulation, or *Zusammenfassung* (system); application, or *Anwendung* (method).

Principle of the five formal steps not new. "However strange the division of teaching according to the formal steps may appear, it is nothing really new, but obtains in every good method of instruction. When based on empiricism alone, it is the result not of psychologic knowledge, but of tact gained by experience, which can produce no convincing proof of its necessity. Through this Herbart-Ziller system of instruction that indefinite feeling is developed into a clear, defined, educational idea. Each single step in the psycho-synthetic building up of the system of education is given in detail and firmly based on psychologic laws.[2] "The formal steps give rule and order to the act of instruction, in accordance with universally recognized laws of the human mind. For a thorough apperception of the material of instruction takes place, only when instruction proceeds from the internal or external observation of the child, proceeds from this to abstract thought, in order finally to ensure the right application of the results of such thought in practical exercises. This methodical procedure, which the nature of the human mind prescribes for us, is also the method of the formal steps."[3]

A Lesson given according to the Five Formal Steps[4]
(age 13 to 14 years).
THE HONEY-BEE (*Apis mellifica* L.).
By Ferdinand Werneburg (Eisenach).

Example of a lesson according to the five formal steps. *Aim.*—We shall learn to-day about the honey-bee. First step: *preparation.*—Before we examine its structure and manner of life more closely, tell me what you already know about it.

---

[1] Association, used both in Herbart's and Rein's terminology, see p. 107, *The Five Formal Steps*.
[2] *Pädagogischer Studien*, Rein.   [3] *On Apperception*, Lange, p. 238.
[4] This lesson is translated from Dr. Schultze's *Deutsche Erziehung*, to which valuable work we are indebted for much material connected with the formal steps.

(A summary of what the children know follows, which is omitted here for want of space.)

Second step: *presentation* of the new.

(I only give the main heads (the concentrations), omitting the combinations (reflections) which follow them, and which are strengthened by looking at live bees and their productions, and by pictures, drawings, and microscopical specimens.)

a. There are three kinds of bee: queen, workers, and drones. Their structure.

b. The bee community and their social life.

c. The religious significance of bees among different nations.

d. The countries, especially in Germany, where honey is now chiefly produced.

Third step: *association*, or formation of concepts.

a. Comparison of the working bee with the queen and the drone (1) in respect to their common, (2) to their diverse characteristics.

b. What difference is there between the wing of the honey-bee and the wing of the cockchafer? (A lesson on the latter had been previously given.)

c. Comparison between these two insects in the structure of the mouth and its parts, and their mode of feeding.

d. Comparison of their mode of development.

Fourth step: *recapitulation*, or system (here the systematic summary of the acquired concepts).

a. Summary (orally) of the chief characteristics of the honey-bee.

b. The pupil writes in his natural history note-book, "The honey-bee belongs to the Hymenoptera; its mouth organs are *masticators* and *lickers*; its development takes place through *metamorphosis*. The product of the egg is a larva without feet, which becomes a puppa, which changes into a perfectly developed insect. Queens and workers possess a *sting*; male bees (the drones) have no such weapon."

Fifth step: *application* of concepts. Oral or written answers to systematically arranged questions, such as the following:—

a. What organs (1) for feeding, (2) for defence, does the bee possess?

b. With what organs does it produce (1) honey; (2) wax?

c. What activity of the bee exhibits a kind of higher mental process?

d. How do you explain the meaning attached to the bee by all nations, especially the ancients?

e. What countries of Europe (1) in ancient times produced, (2) in modern times chiefly produce, honey and wax?

f. From what plants (1) in countries bordering on the Mediterranean Sea, (2) in North Germany, do bees collect the largest amount of honey? (The geographical distribution of the most important plants had been taught in the previous summer term.)

g. Describe the twofold relation of the bee to flowering plants.

How can we, in the light of what we have just said, explain the following poem of Goethe's (æsthetic interest)?—

> "In colours rare
> A flower-bell
> Had early bloomed
> In leafy dell;
> Its sweets to sip
> Bee came to glade:
> Each for the other
> Was surely made."

h. What do you mean by saying, "He is as industrious as a bee"? (moral interest).

i. Draw as seen under the microscope (1) an eye; (2) a foot; (3) the sting of the honey-bee.

k. Draw the front view of a honeycomb, etc. (æsthetic interest).

By this method of teaching, the pupil is raised above mere dogmatic, mechanical, parrot-like learning by rote, and *is taught to think*, to form clear concepts, and to apply them practically. He understands what he has learned, and it can be utilized. Thus this method creates clearness of mind and strength of will. Without these, true morality and strength of character cannot exist. The method, then, is in closest connection with the moral aim of education; both stand in closest connection; the method works towards the aim, and the aim without the method is unattainable.[1]

---

[1] Remarks by Dr. Schultze.

CHAPTER III. (*continued*).

PRACTICAL PEDAGOGY.

SECTION III.—SELECTION OF THE MATERIAL OF INSTRUCTION; THE DUAL THEORY OF THE CONCENTRATION CENTRES AND HISTORICAL CULTURE EPOCHS.

The selection of material. We have already seen that matter which is beyond children's power of comprehension finds too few apperceiving groups of presentations, and consequently excites no interest. Obviously then the *choice* of material must be determined by its adaptability to the apperceptive capacity of the child.

The advocates of the culture epochs claim, that the principle underlying them (1) so determines the selection of the material that it must of necessity be adapted to *each* stage of the child's apperception; (2) that the sequence and co-ordination of the material is ordered by it in such a manner, that a thorough and many-sided *course* of apperception is secured thereby. An examination of all that can be said in favour of and against the theory of the culture epochs, seems to indicate that the application of the principle may secure the second, but leaves the first practically undetermined.

Instruction, we have seen, has to supplement experience and intercourse. From experience we obtain knowledge of the external world, nature; from intercourse our sentiments, our dispositions, towards our fellow-creatures. The Herbartian school, following its founder, who divided instruction into "two main lines, the one for understanding, the other for feeling and imagination,"[1] has thus classified the materials of instruction:—
To supplement experience, instruction uses science matter in the widest sense, which includes geography, natural science in

---

[1] Herbart's fourth letter to Herr von Steiger.

the strict meaning of the word, and mathematics. To supplement intercourse, instruction uses historical-humanistic material, which includes matter for training the disposition: firstly, (*a*) religious history, (*b*) profane history, (*c*) literature; secondly, art matter; and thirdly, language matter.[1] As the worth of the man consists in his disposition, that which trains the disposition best—viz., humanistic subjects—it is urged, ought to take precedence in the school curriculum.

The principle of the selection of material as formulated by Ziller.   The preliminary psychologic conditions of all presentations which are to enter the circle of thought as interesting, is their similarity and relationship to already existing presentations, the latter's expectation, as it were, of their arrival, in short the most careful consideration of the particular individuality and its constantly changing stages of apperception, to which the material must be adapted. The principle as set up by Ziller, the chief representative of the Herbartian school, which is to determine and secure the selection of such material, is contained in the following: "The mental development of the child corresponds in general to the chief phases in the development of his people or of mankind. The mind development of the child therefore cannot be better furthered than when he receives his mental nourishment from the general development of culture, as it is found in literature and history. Every pupil should accordingly pass successively through each of the chief epochs of the general mental development of mankind suitable to his stage of development. The material of instruction therefore should be drawn from the thought material of that stage of historical development in culture, which runs parallel with the present mental state of the pupil." Ziller's principle thus is, in Herbert Spencer's words, that "education should be a repetition of civilisation in little." In other words, every individual must go through each of the stages of development which the race itself has gone through; therefore the best materials for the instruction of the individual are those which represent the main stages of the development of the human race.[2] The question whether this is really a

---
[1] See classification table, p. 101.
[2] This, and the idea of accurately graded instruction, is strictly in

principle upon which the selection and whole arrangement of the material of instruction can be based, or is only a suggestive analogy, opens up at once the contention between the advocates and opponents of the dual theory. Leaving it on one side for the present, we shall give a brief account of the practical working out of the principle by its advocates.

The eight historical culture epochs. In accordance with it, Ziller has selected eight stages called historical culture epochs, corresponding to the eight years of the school course from six to fourteen years. They are—

1. Epic fairy tales.
2. *Robinson Crusoe.*
3. History of the Patriarchs.
4. Judges in Israel.
5. Kings in Israel.
6. Life of Christ.
7. History of the Apostles.
8. History of the Reformation.

Humanistic and scientific instruction must be connected. It must be borne in mind that instruction is to serve the formation of character, and that this is only assured, when a consolidated circle of thought interconnected in all its parts is created. The advocates of the culture epochs urge that, if this is to be done, two wholly independent and separated lines of instruction—viz., the humanistic and scientific—must not be carried on side by side, to form two separate circles of thought. They argue that to avoid this difficulty, nothing remains but to bring them into the closest relationship and connection, and consequently the one material must be more or less determined by the other. To humanistic instruction then, which, as forming the disposition, is to occupy the dominant position, scientific instruction must be joined, and the choice and sequence of the latter must in the main be determined by the former.

---

agreement with Herbert Spencer: "The education of the child must accord both in mode and arrangement with the education of mankind considered historically. In other words the genesis of knowledge in the individual must follow the same course as the genesis of knowledge in the race" (*Education*, p. 67).

Humanistic material to be made the concentration centres. Humanistic and science instruction are combined under one term: "instruction in things" (*Sachunterricht*). In language teaching, things are named and described; in arithmetic, the numbers of things are dealt with; in drawing, things are represented. All these subjects, says Ziller, even including singing, must, if the unity of the circle of thought is to be maintained, be brought into unity with humanistic instruction. The latter, therefore, forms the central point of the whole system of education, and, as with Ziller the treatment of the material of the historical culture epochs is the basis of humanistic instruction, he makes it the *concentration material* for all education.

Principles for the selection of the concentration material. Regarding this Ziller says, "For every grade of instruction and for each class a section of thought complete in itself, a section of humanistic material must be set up as the *concentration centre*, round which all lies peripherally, and from which the connecting threads start which, radiating on all sides continuously, unite and hold together the various parts of the child's circle of thought. In this way instruction ceases to be a loose aggregate of subjects, which otherwise is absolutely unavoidable."

Ziller claims that the choice and sequence of the concentration centres already given are so arranged, that they accord—

(*a*) With the development and progressive culture of the child's mind, that is with the grades of apperception which must succeed each other therein according to psychologic laws.

(*b*) With the development of the child as parallel to the development of the race. All the chief periods of race development important to our present state of culture we know through classical representations; on the contrary, "periods which no master has described, whose spirit no poet breathes, are of little value to education."[1]

Such material of classical representations Ziller gives in his culture epochs. It will be noticed that, although religious instruction is made the centre of education, the two first epochs do not consist of religious matter. Ziller and the modern Her-

---

[1] *Æsthetic Revelation of the World*, p. 74.

bartian school have found that for little children in their two first school years, Bible history is too difficult. The countries and times, with their habits, laws, social forms, etc., are too far removed from the children for them to form any real picture of them. Therefore they consider Bible narratives can only exercise their true influence, if the ground is properly prepared for them during the first two years.

<small>Epic fairy tales as concentration material for the first year.</small> The concentration material therefore, for the first year is not taken from history religious or profane, nor from moral stories, but from stories about real or imaginary beings, *i.e.* from epic fairy tales. These best supply what a child needs. They are simple and yet full of imagination; they are morally cultivating, for they put situations or relationships before the child which call out the moral judgment either in approval or disapproval. They teach much, giving opportunities for conversation on nature and society; they are of permanent value, for they invite a return to them, and make such an impression, that they become a source of many-sided interest. The advantages of this material as summed up by Ziller are as follows: The tales, being poetical, are better suited than anything else to the earliest stage of the child's individuality, when imagination, which needs cultivation because in it all higher aspirations are rooted, is strongest. They are not limited by time and space, for they are often without the names of persons or places. The child lives in them beyond the limits of the material, makes the dead living, puts a soul into the soulless, and has intercourse with the whole world as his equal. This has no bad influence on him, for the tales contain, beside their subjective view of things, a number of objective æsthetic and ethical ideas and principles consonant with reason. These serve specially to exercise the ethical judgment, as the tales open out a large field where many true and simple cases come before the child, upon which he can decide easily, quickly, and clearly. As he grows older, and his experience becomes richer, the real in the tales is less cared for, and more interest is taken in the poetical and ideal truth of the æsthetic and ethical, which thus remains as a residue much to be desired, giving an ideal direction to the thoughts, and a

higher activity to the intellectual life.¹ If the child came in the tales in contact with nothing but actual realities, his mind would soon become open only to the commonest sensuous impressions, and would have neither sensibility nor receptivity for poetry, nor for the wonder and reverence which is a part of religion. Again, all education must start from the individual, but with the aim of raising the pupil above his individuality, of correcting the tendency of imagination to centre in self, by placing him amidst general human relationships. "For the beginning of moral culture, weak and uncertain in itself, will be interfered with by everything that makes the individual self the point of reference for the world outside it."² This danger these tales tend to prevent. They widen out the child's consciousness from self to those about him, from the local to the national, and from the national to all mankind; they lead him into sympathy with that childlike spirit which was a characteristic of the childhood of the race; they are a sure means of creating ethical judgment and religious feeling in the simplest relationships within the child's sphere of apperception. The modern Herbartian school—Ziller, Rein, Pickel, Staude, and others—have created a literature on this subject, to which we refer the reader who desires to study it further.

"Robinson Crusoe" as concentration material for the second year. The concentration material for the second year must be chosen on the one hand so as to continue the awakened activity of the imagination, and yet on the other, by a definite relation to history, prepare to limit its unbounded activity, and lead the pupil to an apprehension

---

¹ Froebel constantly recognizes the same fact: that through material which appeals to the child's imagination, he may gradually be led most easily from the sensuous to the ideal. In the song of "The Joiner" the idea of contrast (between his long and short strokes) is further brought out in the picture attached to it of the long "giant Goliath, who plays such a laughably important rôle in the child-world, and dear little David, with whom children always sympathize so warmly." But both song and picture contain beyond an ideal truth which through them the child will see. "The little picture wants to lead your child early to the idea that outer greatness by no means always implies inner greatness, and that the converse of this is true also" (Froebel's *Mutter und Kose Lieder*, No. 40, translated by Frances and Emily Lord).

² *Science of Education*, p. 246.

of historical development. The new material must be such as can be used to spin further the threads already fastened, which are to be woven into the material of a moral-religious character. This is found, says Ziller, in Defoe's *Robinson Crusoe*.[1] For, he urges, it takes the child back to those prehistoric times when man alone, without society, raised himself through want and difficulties above nature, to master and use it for his ends; it takes him to those times, when the simplest and most necessary experiences were gained and things invented, the value of which we now through constant use hardly realize. Without that realization, however, the human mind could not have passed onward to those sociological ideas which were necessary to the development of its historic sense. If this point has been gained, the pupil's "chronological progress from the old to the new"[2] enjoined by Herbart is possible. In Ziller's culture epochs, that progress from the end of the second year, is from the earliest history of Palestine to the present day.

Materials for the third and succeeding years. The concentration material for the third year is the history of the Patriarchs, as the earliest representatives of human culture; that for the fourth year is the heroes, the Judges, in Israel; for the fifth year the kings, as representing an ordered state organism. For the sixth year, the life of Jesus, the view of life embodied in Him is an epoch in the general development of culture, which, according to Ziller, corresponds, or should correspond, to the child's development. The two last epochs (the history of the Apostles and of the Reformation) are considered necessary as showing the spread, the personal acquirement by, and embodiment of the Christian idea in the people, and they are also

---

[1] The educational value of *Robinson Crusoe* was thus estimated by Rousseau: "Since we must have books, there is one which to my mind furnishes the finest of treatises on education according to nature. My Émile shall read this book before any other; it shall for a long time be his entire library, and shall always hold an honourable place. It shall be the text, on which all our discussions of natural science shall be only commentaries; it shall be a test for all we meet during our progress toward a ripened judgment, and so long as our taste is unspoiled we shall enjoy reading it. What wonderful book is this—Aristotle? Pliny? Buffon? No; it is *Robinson Crusoe*" (Rousseau's *Émile*, Book III.). [2] *Science of Education*, p. 181.

of value for grounding the pupils further in the spirit of Christianity.

Parallel material from German history attached to the centres. Parallel to the history of the Israelites, that of the Germans is placed, and in such a way that each corresponding epoch is entered upon contemporaneously. The patriarchal times, for instance, are parallel with the Thuringian sagas, the Judges with the Siegfried sagas, and with the times of the kings in Israel, the times of the Kaisers in Germany (Karl the Great; Barbarossa). Parallel with the life of Jesus is placed that of the great Reformer Luther, and with the first spread of Christianity that of the spread and consolidation of Protestantism.

This material taken from great epochs is calculated to fill the pupil's mind worthily, and it will be enriched by a further series. Material connected with it from German literature will be added to the concentration material. Thus for German pupils, the time of Charles the Great will be introduced by the Rolands and Karl sagas. Many subjects must be selected from the realms of nature and art, which are necessary to the due understanding of the concentration material. Geography especially must be closely connected with it. The lives of the Patriarchs and of Jesus cannot be made living representations, unless instruction is given in the geography, natural history, climate, soil, of Palestine, its inhabitants, their habits and employments. As already explained, the child's *existent* store of ideas and experiences must be connected with, and used to elucidate, wherever possible, the new material of the culture epochs.

A grave objection, which will be considered later in more detail, to the dual theory, naturally suggests itself at this point. Its opponents contend that the connection between the concentration and other material cannot be maintained. This the adherents of the theory unhesitatingly deny. They, moreover, affirm that the subjects do not lose their essential characteristics, nor become mere appendages of the concentration material, because *connecting points* only are made between the different branches. The material of each subject is treated by the method best suited to it, and a well-connected circle of thought is created in the child's mind. That such a treatment is possible, the Ziller practising school in Leipsic has, in Ufer's opinion, clearly proved.[1]

In Chapter III., section 5, the concentration and secondary material for a series of lessons in culture epoch 6 (age 11 to 12) is given, and, where necessary, English material is suggested in place of the German.

General remarks on the dual theory. It is important for the reader to grasp clearly the dual theory described in the foregoing pages, of the concentration centres and the historical culture grades as elaborated and formulated by Ziller and other modern Herbartians, and advocated at the present time by Prof. Rein, of Jena, by Ufer, and others. They propose to carry on the practical work of education by its aid, and to remodel the elementary school system thereon, while using the "formal steps," which are certainly Herbart's, as the psychologic working out of the process of apperception in the details of instruction.

The dual theory not Herbart's. Let it be clearly understood, however, that this dual theory is *not* Herbart's, nor was it originated by him. On the contrary, it has been developed since his death by his before-named followers. Some of the ideas lying at its root may indeed be found in the germ in his writings, but he must not be held responsible for it.

As a tentative attempt to base instruction on the process of apperception agreeably to psychologic laws, and at the same time, as Voigt points out, to supply the real need of a right principle for the choice and ordering of the material of instruction, this theory is most interesting, and practical attempts to work it out will claim the attention of teachers and those concerned in education. Its application to school work in Germany has not yet gone beyond the stage of experiment. Time and experience only can demonstrate how much true psychologic value it possesses. Although Herbart's principles are quietly

---

[1] Ziller's *Grundlegung zur Lehre vom erziehenden Unterricht* (1865) contains this theory, and Prof. Rein, of Jena, Pickel and Scheller in Eisenach, have worked it out practically in their *Theorie und Praxis des Volksschulunterrichts nach Herbartischen Grundsätzen*, an epoch-making work in the history of education. Ziller's practising school in Leipsic is no longer in existence.

exercising an increasing influence on educational methods in Germany, this theory has at present only been worked out in the practising school at Jena under Prof. Rein, who is a lecturer at the university there.

A curriculum based on the dual theory. To enable the reader to understand the practical method proposed to be adopted in working it out, a curriculum and time-table based on it are given, which were submitted in November, 1893, by a committee of teachers, to the School Board of Würzburg, for their approval and for adoption in the elementary schools of that city. One of the members of this committee writes to us that this plan, "based wholly," he says, "on Herbart-Ziller principles, may be considered as an additional stone in their system, and that the requirements formulated therein are grounded on the practical experience of its authors" (*i.e.*, the committee). The curriculum and time-table, however, were as such not adopted by the Board, but many of the recommendations will be carried out.

Difficulties in the practice of the dual theory. Referring the reader to the curriculum and time-table in the preceding pages, he will observe that the historical culture grades, each with its concentration centre, represent the spinal column of the whole system. It may be imagined as the *vertical* line in the order of time, starting from the first school year and running upwards to the last, while the various subjects of instruction radiate *horizontally*; these start from the concentration centres, and are thus to be connected with each other and the centre by the process of apperception, forming thereby, it is said, a "united circle of thought."

In this plan the historical culture grades are contained in columns 1 and 2, and the religious historical material forming them dominates the other subjects, which are to be connected by apperception with the centre and with each other.[1]

In teaching on this system, there are thus three continuous and separate lines to be followed :—

---

[1] It will be noticed that on the first attempt to carry out this theory practically its main principle—viz., *one* series of centres from which all shall start—broke down, and it was found necessary to adopt *two* series of historical grades, one religious and the other secular.

Mark Finchlestein stole this page

Jan. 2/74

Firstly, the process of apperception must be carried on vertically from year to year in each subject; secondly, the same process must be carried on horizontally through all the subjects in each year; and yet lastly, at the same time, the due development of each subject year by year must also be provided for.

For instance, arithmetic must begin in the first year with the very simplest exercises in the counting of 1 to 10, and gradually grow wider each year, till it includes decimal fractions, etc.; and yet, while thus growing wider, the material of each lesson must be connected apperceptively in each year with the concentration centre of that year, and with all the other subjects, also growing wider of that year on the horizontal line. Each subject must grow *pari passu* with the others, and yet as each grows, the appercepting connecting links must be maintained along the line horizontally from the centre to the extremest point, and vertically with what has gone before and what comes after.

Can subjects having no natural affinity be connected apperceptively? and even if this be possible, can the connections be maintained as the lines extend vertically in years and growth, and horizontally in subjects branching out year by year, which become more technical and special as they grow? Will not the connections become looser and more indefinite as the length of the lines from centre to subject, and subject to subject horizontally, and from year to year vertically, increases, till they are as good as lost altogether? This is the crux of the whole theory. If feasible, it stands; if not, it breaks down altogether. We give at the close of Chapter III., section 4, a critique on this dual theory by G. Voigt, taken from a monograph by him on "The Importance of Herbart's Pedagogy for the Elementary School."[1] While adopting Herbart's principles in the main, he rejects this theory altogether.

Dörpfeld, a great school authority in Germany, is certainly no upholder of the historical culture grades. He points out they

---

[1] *Die Bedeutung der Herbartischen Pädagogik für die Volksschule*, G. Voigt (R. Neumeister, Schönebeck, Prussia).

are not conceptually a part of the concentration principle, of which latter he would strive to secure the general adoption. He requires, firstly, each subject to form a united whole; secondly, all subjects to be connected according to their nature; thirdly, the central position of religious instruction in the service of the formation of character and culture of the disposition. This leaves it open to form *several* concentration centres, around which the material of instruction may be grouped according to natural affinity. Voigt makes a similar suggestion at the close of his monograph just referred to.

Religious material for the concentration centres discussed in the light of Herbart's ethical aim. Before leaving this part of our subject it may be remarked in conclusion, that this theory would seem to be the indirect outcome of the attempt made, and still being made, by the modern Herbartian school, to get Herbart's principles adapted to elementary education. The system of methodic units used in the treatment of the material of instruction, as adapted by the modern school is undoubtedly based on Herbart's educational psychology. They claim that this dual theory is so also, but it may be doubted if such be the case, and even if so, it may be doubted still more whether Herbart would have worked it out in this form. Herbart himself, when teaching Herr von Steiger's boys in Switzerland, really used, though not ostensibly, Homer and the Greek writers as concentration centres. The great aim of the present Herbartian leaders is to get, as before stated, his principles carried out in the elementary school system of Germany. This would be a hopeless task without direct religious instruction. They have, therefore, elaborated this dual theory and made formal religious instruction the backbone of the whole system, by using religious material for the concentration centres in each historical culture grade except the two first, in the interest, it is said, "of the formation of character." The question may be asked, Would not Herbart himself have worked it out on purely ethical lines, using Greek history in the place of Jewish, and the history of Christ and Christianity in a simple, non-sectarian spirit? The principle lying at the root of the concentration centres may probably be found in the germ in Herbart, and has much to recommend it; but as to its working out and the material needed for it, much difference of opinion may, and does, come in. The Roman Catholic could, and certainly would, work the dual theory on Roman Catholic lines; Anglicans, Jews, Mahometans, would each use it to centralize his own religion, and each would adapt the history selected, for his own purpose and read into it his own meaning. This applicability of the dual theory to different and intrinsically opposed educational aims would seem to indicate that there is psychologic truth in it, probably in the concentration centres. The difference between Herbart and the modern school becomes at once apparent by comparing their aims. The aim of education as defined by him is the formation of a moral character, as we have before shown; that of the latter is also the formation of a moral character, but *plus* that of a sound Lutheran Christian.

In a small treatise by Dr. Thrändorf on "The Treatment of Religious Instruction according to the Herbart-Ziller Method,"[1] this is worked out, and carried to the point of preparing the pupil on leaving school for confirmation and entrance into the Lutheran Church. The whole course proposed in this treatise is of the most dogmatic, sectarian character. Herbart, although a deeply religious man himself, practically excluded direct dogmatic religious teaching from the school aim, as belonging to the province of the home and the Church. For doing this and limiting the "aim" to the formation of a moral character, he had cogent reasons, reasons bound up with his whole theory of education. He desired that education should attain certitude in its aim, means, and results, and that a moral character should be formed which later on, when the work of the school was over, would withstand the storms of passion and temptations of life, based firmly as on a rock. For the means, he uses psychology. The aim—ethics—he bases also on what he considers an impregnable rock, viz., the intuitive judgments of the mind.

---

[1] *Die Behandlung des Religions-Unterrichts nach Herbart-Zillersche Methode*, Dr. Thrändorf (A. Beger and Söhne, Langensalza).

Nothing that can come in after-life can shake this ethical basis, and being interwoven with the whole circle of thought, the stability of the character is assured. But if in the place of this aim another, the formation of a specific Lutheran Christian or of a Roman Catholic, is placed, the centre of gravity is shifted from a rock to a weaker foundation.[1] For while different religions are based on different foundations all more or less laid in faith, foundations which in after-life may be, and constantly are, undermined by currents of new and wider knowledge and deeper insight, the purely moral aim rests secure on its own indestructible basis. To make then religious material the matter of the concentration centres, which are the spinal column of the whole system, from which all starts and upon which all rests, would seem to be peculiarly dangerous. For if, when the pupil has arrived at intellectual maturity, and tests the grounds of all he has been taught, he finds them partly untenable, and must give up some, then the whole building of the circle of thought will be shaken to its centre, and the very foundations of his mind be torn up.[2] For if even only some of the acquired religious principles have gone overboard, they, having formed part of the concentration centres, will in coming down dislocate other principles acquired at the same time through apperception, and will either bring them down too, or leave them without support. Anyway in such cases, the unity of the circle of thought upon which stability of character rests will be broken into, and the harmony thus disturbed will hardly ever be regained.

These reasons would seem to be sufficient to account for Herbart's limitation of the aim of education to the formation of a moral character, one, however, he presupposes to be interwoven with a simple faith in the fatherhood and love of God, in His ruling providence, and in the hope of immortality, whereby our relation to Him as children is realized. These simple truths lie at the basis of all religions, and to this extent

---

[1] These and the adherents of nearly all other religions base their ethics on religious dogmas.
[2] Such a catastrophe is vividly described in *Robert Elsmere*.

Herbart would go, making an atmosphere of them in which the child should grow up. His idea of religion as bound up in the aim of education, and the manner in which it should be taught, can be gathered from that section of synthetic instruction entitled "Religion" in the *Science of Education* (pp. 179-187), to which we refer the reader.

CHAPTER III. (continued)

PRACTICAL PEDAGOGY

SECTION IV.—VOIGT'S CRITICISM ON THE DUAL THEORY AS APPLIED TO INSTRUCTION IN ELEMENTARY SCHOOLS

Voigt fully accepts the main principles of Herbart's pedagogy, and is of opinion that, if they are generally carried out, the elementary school system of Germany will be still further perfected and extended. Yet none the less can he approve of this new development, elaborated he says, by some modern followers of Herbart, and which has found expression in the idea of this dual theory as applied to the work of instruction.

This development starts from the idea, that the first aim of all education is to form the disposition (*Gesinnung*[1]). For this purpose, suitable material is required. This material must be of a moral-religious nature, because the moral-religious relationships are of paramount influence in forming character and disposition. Its form must be historical, the individual being the basis of the general, and also because history, especially religious history, is best adapted to awake the "whole of interest."

Hence arises the necessity of finding a principle which shall determine the choice of the material, a necessity which suggests further the question, whether an objective principle at all can be found for this choice. Such a principle the advocates of this theory think they have found in the supposed fact that an agreement exists between the development the individual and the development the human race has gone through in their various successive stages. From this the conclusion is drawn,

---

[1] *Gesinnung*. The English language has no equivalent for this word. We use "disposition" as the nearest, but it must include all that goes to make up the character of a man, both as to strength and nature, as to his opinions, feelings, and views of life.

that for each development stage of the child, the needful material of instruction is to be found in the parallel development stage of the race; consequently certain historical culture grades must be worked through in each school year, and the choice of the material will be determined accordingly.

As to the actual building up of these grades, the choice of suitable material for them, and the epochs from which it should be taken, much difference of opinion exists amongst the advocates of the theory themselves. Voigt goes on to describe the material hitherto proposed to be used, which need not be repeated here, as it agrees with the account already given in the preceding pages.[1]

Thus far only one side of this dual theory has been explained; let us turn to the other. If, it is argued, the material to be used in forming the disposition is to acquire in the pupil's mind, that preponderating weight and clearness which is needful to secure permanently the unity of the disposition, the other subjects of instruction must not be taught independently of this material. On the contrary, it must be made the dominating *middle point* (concentration centre) of the whole course of instruction, so that all the other subjects lie around it peripherally, and are subordinated to it in choice and treatment. They will rest on it, and be treated in connection with it, for only in this way (such is the view of the advocates of the theory) will instruction cease to be a mere aggregate of loose subjects. Only in this way can the central dominating position of the moral-religious ideas in the circle of thought be secured, and thereby the unity of the disposition be firmly established.

Whatever truth this dual theory may contain, it will be found to be untenable in the form proposed, whether, firstly, we consider the way in which right ideas of Herbart's have been theoretically developed, or, secondly, examine the grounds out of which they have grown, or, lastly, look at the manner in which they have been carried out in practical instruction.

Three ideas of Herbart's are sought to be utilized in this theory. The first is, All instruction should work as a cultivat-

---

[1] See pp. 123-128.

ing activity; the second, All instruction should develop interest; the third, All instruction should create connected masses of presentations. These three thoughts clearly dominate the whole conception. It is, however, equally clear that they are worked out, either in an exaggerated form or in a superficial manner, and for the following reasons:—

When Herbart says, All instruction should aim at forming the will, he does not mean that it should everywhere direct the will *immediately* on the good. On the contrary, he shows that the *mediate* formation of the will, which every good system of instruction serves, is the right and quite indispensable method. But the gist of the method implied in this theory lies in trying to direct the will immediately and constantly on the good, and demands for this purpose that the material specially suited thereto, should externally dominate the whole course of instruction. This is carrying out in a strained and exaggerated manner, a right principle.

Again, when it is said, All instruction should develop interest, it cannot possibly be intended that every method unit (lesson) should set the whole of interest in movement at once. All that can be required is, that each unit shall awake that interest which is cognate to the subject under treatment, and that thus in the due course of instruction the whole circle of interest will be cared for. It has been shown, too, that the interest attached to knowledge (*Erkenntniss*) is also of decisive importance in the formation of the will. What ground is there, then, for treating this class of material as of secondary rank in comparison with that attached to sympathy, or for trying quite unnecessarily to raise the former in a manner to its full value, by connecting it in a mere external way with the moral-religious material selected for the formation of the disposition?

Lastly, even if the aim of instruction be to create connected masses of presentations, it cannot be intended that all presentations created by instruction should form a *single mass*, which nevertheless would still be wanting in true inner connection. On the contrary, it is more in harmony with this principle of Herbart's, that several such centres or masses should be created, provided only that connected groups of presentations grow around such centres. Voigt goes still farther, and maintains that, as Herbart distinguishes between different kinds of interest, dividing it into two main lines,[1] such a formation in groups is necessary, and he thinks that in this direction a new and valuable development of present educational methods for elementary schools can be made.

Having thus shown that right ideas of Herbart have been misapplied in working out this dual theory, we shall again on examination find, that the grounds or presumptions out of which it has grown, are partly false and partly unproven.

For is it not clearly an error to imagine that a mere external artificial concentration—and such only is possible when, for instance, instruction in arithmetic and natural history is tacked on subordinately to the moral-religious material—is it not an error to think that such a concentration possesses any value for the cultivation of the circle of thought, to say nothing of the formation of the will? To connect what in its nature is related, is right, and of the highest importance, not only for intellectual training, but also for the general culture of the man. But when the attempt is made to forcibly connect what is not related, apperception does not take place; the opposite of unity—namely, dispersion—ensues, even of that which in itself has true inward affinity.

Again, the second presumption, and the one most closely bound up with Herbart's fundamental principles, from which this idea of the dual theory has sprung, is that the power with which the presentations act on the will depends only on their formal connection and on their being bound up in masses hanging together. This presumption is in two respects wrong: firstly, because the volitions are not a necessary result of the mechanical course of the presentations, and therefore they *alone* cannot be the determining power which causes the movements of the will; and, secondly, apart from the limits drawn by the freedom of the will, the preponderance of certain groups of presentations cannot determine the soul merely by their formal

---

[1] Viz., interest as growing out of knowledge and of sympathy. See *Science of Education*, p. 133.

order. As the soul is not a void, but primordially rich with living powers, the force or weight of the presentations is also determined by their nature or contents. The soul is originally predisposed to the good, the ideal, and it is this inborn affinity with the good, which gives the moral-religious presentations the possibility of rising to a certain power, quite as much as does the method of their preparation and connection. If this be the case, then, it cannot possibly be a right method of teaching for the teacher to be *constantly* impressing these (moral-religious) ideas on the child; only when he does so, he must do it with clearness, authority, and emphasis.

Our objections so far have been directed against the idea of the concentration centres, but they have practically touched that of the historical culture grades as well. For both ideas stand in such relationship that the concentration idea can be accepted independently, as it says in itself nothing regarding the nature of the presumed centres. The idea of the historical culture grades, on the other hand, loses its importance unless it stands in connection with the concentration centres. But notwithstanding this, our objections are not exhausted till we have examined the principle of the historical culture grades by itself, and its claims on our approval.

The philosophical ground on which this theory rests—viz., that there is a law of parallelism between the development of the individual and that of the race—is a pleasing idea; but, carefully looked at, it turns out to be nothing but an *unproved assertion*. On this ground alone, it is unsuited to fix the normal course of instruction. It will further be found to be *false* when it is remembered that this parallelism, if such exist, applies to the *whole* of a human lifetime, while it is here applied to the mere limits of childhood, and to the course of a few school years only. This alone is fatal to the application of the idea to educational purposes. In what possible sense can it be said that a child in the limits of his individual school-life can go through the development stages of the human race? Whatever can be brought forward in support of this idea, it is in any case inconsequent to limit its application to the years of childhood, and with this all grounds in its favour are destroyed.

In addition to this, there are other serious objections against the idea itself, objections which, in whatever way it may be practically carried out in the school, must necessarily cause its rejection.

Firstly, it is maintained that a child should historically go through—*i.e.*, live into—the various epochs of human development and culture. Is it not then a strange inconsistency, when tracing before the child the religious development of the race, to begin with the monotheistic stage of the Old Testament? Ought not a beginning to be made with earlier, more imperfect forms, which find expression in the heathen conceptions of the universe, in shapes from the rudest and most primordial to the noblest and purest? It is besides totally insufficient to use the Israelite race only, as transmitters historically of the development of culture, for in regard to art and science they accomplished so little, and are not to be compared with the Greeks. If this idea, then, is to be seriously carried out, a compendious history of religions, besides the Old Testament grade referred to, must be worked out, and with it at least the development of the Greeks. But as this is a work from which the boldest educational idealist would shrink, it is quite clear that for elementary schools at any rate the idea is impracticable.

We are led to the same decided rejection when we consider historical culture development, not in its extension, but in regard to its matter and contents. The development of human culture is presented in external history only in an attenuated form, for it has been determined mainly by the progressive culture of the mind, realized in religion, philosophy, science, and art. These, however, are matters which lie almost totally beyond the comprehension of school-children, and must remain so.

The impossibility, therefore, is thus clearly to be seen of adapting this idea for the purposes of elementary education with any truth or success whatever.

Such an adaptation would, in addition, be entirely opposed to one of the most important of Herbart's principles.[1] It is a pure

---

[1] Voigt seems here to overlook Herbart's repeatedly expressed thought that the subject matter best suited to a boy's psychologic state of de-

fiction, totally incompatible with the power and importance of the process of apperception, to imagine that a child of the present stands inwardly nearer to the time of the infancy of the race, than he does to the relationships of his own time. In consequence of the given apperceiving presentations which are constantly moulding the life of the child, that life is rooted in the *present*, and for the purposes of this theory, must be transferred thence into the strange relationships of a distant past. The German empire is to the German child a clear presentation full of apperceiving power; his idea of the patriarchal social constitution, on the contrary, is in comparison a misty conception. Modern life, with its railways, telegraphs, steamers, and factories, presents itself clearly before his eyes; the imperfect social life of primitive stages of culture, passed over long ago, is, on the contrary, quite strange to him. How then can it be maintained with any degree of reason that an elementary school child should go through the whole series of the development grades of human culture, in order at the end to come out at the present?

Do not let us deceive ourselves. This idea of the parallelism of general and individual development is a theoretical idea, which belongs to historical science, and that only. It is a mistake to build the work of education, which has to serve practical ends, upon such an unproven, misty conception. Life only vivifies in contact with life; but the life of the child is in the *present*, which bears within itself the main products of all past culture. It is therefore sufficient to offer the child the most valuable results of the long past both in the spheres of religion and of secular knowledge, and give so much of past history as is needful for a sympathetic understanding of the present.

It remains now only to show that the combination of both these ideas is impracticable. A detailed proof, however, is

velopment is to be found in the history of the childhood of the Greek race, and not in his own times. This thought is clearly given in his introduction to the *Science of Education* (p. 89). Had he considered such subject matter unsuitable for apperception, he would not have enjoined " a chronological progress from the old to the new " (*Science of Education*, p. 181).

superfluous; all that is needed is to point to the various attempts made to carry them out. Such attempts are inevitably doomed to failure, as in their practical working out the band which should tie the individual subjects together (apperceptively) becomes looser with every additional step outwards from the concentration centre. To the moral-religious material forming the concentration centres, a second—viz., the national—is added during the course; and thus the ground idea of the whole theory, which demands absolute external unity, is wholly given up, and a series of dual centres is created. The connection of the individual subjects with one or other of these two centres, grows gradually looser the longer the chain becomes, till at last it is dropped altogether, and no attempt is made to keep even the two centres in real relation to each other. We can thus say that, so far as present experience reaches, the idea of the historical culture grades and concentration centres has not yet been shown to be capable of practical realization.

While thus rejecting this dual theory, Voigt points out that it has arisen from a real need, viz., to find out a true and thoroughgoing principle for the choice and ordering of the material of instruction. Although it has not proved equal to solving this problem, the future satisfactory progress of the elementary schools will depend on the way in which this question is dealt with. It will also depend on whether the dangers bound up with the dispersion of the circle of thought which results from present methods of instruction can be warded off, dangers which must necessarily increase with the increase of knowledge and of subjects.

This theory contains, as before stated, three aims: first, that connected masses of presentations be created; second, that the material of instruction be grouped round a central point; and third, that the central moral-religious material be made to follow the course of the cultural development of the race. The two last of these are rejected as untenable, but the first deserves serious consideration. Voigt then goes on to show in detail how present methods of instruction directly tend to hinder the growth of interconnected masses of presentations. The textbooks in use, too, have the same influence. A concentration therefore of the material of instruction *is a great need*; but to concentrate all under *one* centre has already been shown to be impossible, especially to make historical material this centre. He therefore suggests the question whether, as the interest to be awakened by instruction follows two main lines, it is not desirable to divide the material into two main groups, according as it relates to the interests of knowledge or of sympathy. Then by their side the higher and manual arts would form a third group, aiming at developing the creative powers of the individual, as well as awakening æsthetic interest. These groups would be carried along parallel lines through the whole school course, each independently in the way its own nature requires. But in each individual group, for each grade of instruction, only one province interconnected in itself would be treated, so that the group would gradually be built up out of the sum of these units. It certainly, for instance, would be incomparably better to teach the pupil national history daily in one year instead of twice a week in six years. In this way then the requirement would be satisfied which lies at the root of this dual theory, while the faults attaching to it would be avoided.

The reader desirous of pursuing this subject further is referred to Prof. Rein's work *Outlines of Pedagogics*,[1] where he will find a full explanation of the theory and all that can be said in its favour. Prof. Rein is its most enthusiastic exponent in Germany. On the other hand, he is strongly recommended to study Lange's careful and judicial examination of the subject in his work before referred to on apperception.[2] In the section on "The Choice and Arrangement of the Material of Instruction" he submits this theory to a psychologic analysis, and shows therein that it is untenable, although containing some germs of truth.

---

[1] Pp. 93-135. Translated by C. C. and Ida van Liew (Swan Sonnenschein & Co.).

[2] *Apperception: a Monograph on Psychology and Pedagogy* (Heath & Co.), pp. 109-150.

CHAPTER III. (*continued*)

PRACTICAL PEDAGOGY

SECTION V.—EXAMPLES OF LESSONS BASED ON THE THEORY OF THE CONCENTRATION CENTRES AND HISTORICAL CULTURE EPOCHS

We have seen that, by the dual theory, education of the disposition (*Gesinnungsunterricht*) or, as Herbart calls it, education of the heart, must occupy the central place in the plan of instruction. For each school year, the material chosen must illustrate the development of the race, and as such, it is alleged, must necessarily be parallel with the development of the individual, *i.e.* with his power of apperception.

Religious matter for the sixth school year, (for pupils eleven to twelve years old) is the life of Jesus. Parallel to it are the voyages of discovery, and (suggested for an English table as a substitute for the life of Luther in the German) the life of Wiclif, the great English Reformer.

Between the life of Jesus and the life of Wiclif there are many points of connection. Those which can be made between the life of Jesus and the voyages of discovery are fewer; *i.e.*, Christ broke through the Jewish tribal limitation of the kingdom of God to the nation; the heathen throughout the world were to have their share of heaven. The voyages of discovery point "to the people still sitting in darkness." The sending out of the disciples suggests the missions of Christian nations to the heathen, and with that, the contrast between the self-sacrificing love of Christ, and the self-seeking of those who taught in His name.

The following subjects Ufer has, in accordance with the dual theory, treated as described. Where necessary, however, the material in use in German schools has been exchanged by the authors for such as could be used in England.[1]

---

[1] See Rein's *Classification of Educative Instruction*, p. 104.

ENGLISH.

a. *Material for reading:* The Evangelists; Dr. Geikie's *Life of Christ*; Washington Irving's *Life of Columbus*; Cabot's *Voyages*; Kingsley's *Westward Ho!* Longman's *Life of Wiclif*; Chaucer's *Prologue*; Pauli's *Pictures of Old England*; Palgrave's *The Merchant and the Friar*.

b. *Poetry* (love as the soul of Christ and of Christianity): "The Vision of Sir Launfal," by Russell Lowell; "The Legend of St. Christopher," by Lewis Morris; "Building of the Ship," by Longfellow; "Columbus," by Russell Lowell,
        leading to

England's settlement of religious liberty beyond the seas. Connected poems are "Bermuda," by Andrew Marvel, *Moravian Missions* from James Montgomery's poem "The West Indies," this again
        leading to

England's mission of civilization, in connection with "Slavery," from Cowper's *Task*; "Stanzas to Freedom," by Russell Lowell; "Freedom," by Tennyson.

In connection with the Spaniards' intercourse with the Indians, extracts from Longfellow's "Hiawatha" may be read. Columbus sailed the sea, description of which, its bottom, inhabitants, etc., are treated under other heads. But with this may be here connected "The Sailor's Grave"; Byron's "Hymn to the Ocean" (*Childe Harold*, Canto 4); "The Treasures of the Deep" (Mrs. Hemans); Clarence's dream (Shakespeare, *Richard III.*, Act I., Scene 4); Psalm cvii. 23-30, beginning "They that go down to the sea in ships."

As a picture of Wiclif, "the poure persone of a toun," Prologue; Chaucer's *Canterbury Tales*.

c. *English composition:*—
    1. A short prose narration of the legend of St. Christopher.
    2. Description of Drake's ship the *Pelican*.
    3. When the reading of "Columbus" is finished, the pupils must sketch the outlines of the hero's character on definite lines: industry, perseverance, trust in God, courage; some or all of such to be worked into compositions.

4. Further material for composition will be obtained from geography and natural science.

d. The corrections in composition supply material for instruction in *grammar*; errors in punctuation, for instance, suggest treatment of the simpler forms of the complex sentence, and the differences between them and compound sentences.

e. *The history of literature* takes the biography of Longfellow, which can easily be connected with his poem, and the biography of Goldsmith, as reflected in "The Vagabond" and "The Traveller."

f. *Prosody.* The poem "Columbus" may be treated as an example of *blank verse* (used also by Shakespeare, Wordsworth, and Tennyson):—

Hyperbole—"A hand is stretched to him from out the dark."
Alliteration—"The cordage creaks and rattles;"
"The sigh of some grim monster undescried;"
"The wicked and the weak."

In connection with "The Sailor's Grave," instances of *crossed rhymes*:—

"There is in the lone, lone sea
A spot unmarked, but holy;
For there the gallant and the free
In his ocean bed lies lowly."

In connection with "Stanzas to Freedom,"—

Elegiacs—"They are slaves who dare not be
In the right with two or three."
Polysyndeton—"They sleep a calm and peaceful sleep."

As in "The Building of the Ship" "plied" and "side," "force" and "course" rhyme, the pupil sees rhyme is determined, not by eye, as he would probably suppose, but by ear.

GEOGRAPHY.

The voyages of Columbus lead to a more detailed consideration of the sea, which may be connected with what the children have already learned on the same subject in *Robinson Crusoe*. We may consider—

Open and inland seas;
Colour and motion of the sea;
Taste of sea-water, salt deserts.

Boys may take a more detailed description of a ship, and here again there is connected material in *Robinson Crusoe*.

Columbus sailed the Atlantic Ocean. The name suggests the fabled Atlantis and its remains, which are supposed still to exist in several groups of islands.

Pieces of pumice stone are found floating at sea. This fact leads to the volcanic nature of the sea-bottom, and particularly to the description of groups of islands of volcanic origin.

The Lesser Antilles.

Columbus touched first at the *Canary Isles*, and later landed on an island of the *Bahama Group* (compare natural history material).

The fact that the Spaniards made settlements on the *Greater Antilles*, leads to a description of these islands. The treasures which Columbus sent as proofs of his successful discoveries, give occasion to treat of the significance of the Greater Antilles in the world's commerce (compare natural science material).

After considering the West Indies, the name of which is explained by reference to Columbus's voyages, we may pass to

The North American Mainland,

the middle and northern parts of which will be described, while the southern part will be left till the discovery and conquest of Mexico are treated of.

The poem "Hiawatha" supplies connecting points for considering the Indians: form, character, religion, modes of life, habits, and customs.

The poem "Bermuda" leads to a description of the farmer's life and occupations (emigrants; primeval forests; prairies).

As a contrast, the consideration of social and commercial life in great towns (wealth; luxury; industry) may be taken in this connection.

Commercial intercourse between the old and new worlds leads to a notice of the means of intercourse: Steamers, Transatlantic Cable, Pacific Railway, etc.

On his last voyage, Columbus tried to find a passage through Central America from the Atlantic to the Pacific Ocean. This leads to the description of the land, and to the mention of the commencement of the Panama Canal (engineer; comparison with Suez Canal: the use of both).

The idea Columbus had of reaching India from the west, must be understood together with the spherical shape of the earth. This is the connecting point for astronomical geography, as also are the trade winds, sea currents, degrees of warmth, eclipse of the moon, all of which find a place in the voyages of Columbus.

NATURAL HISTORY.

a. Description of natural features.

Columbus found in the Saragossa Sea large masses of sea-weed.
1. Description of unicellular seaweed.
2. General description of marine vegetation.

The fact that the seaweed is torn from its place of growth and sinks, leads to the

Origin of Coal.

The carbonization of wood fibre in a piece of wood, which has been kept by water from contact with air, is shown. An excursion should be made to a turf or coal-pit, if possible.

Consideration of the difference between black coal, brown coal, and peat, with reference to their origin.

The Bahama Islands, on which Columbus landed, are coral islands; therefore here follows

A Description of Organ Coral.

With the description of these islands formed by coral, can be connected that of the

Precious or Blood Coral,

as well as other valuable productions of the sea-bottom, viz., *the pearl-shell*—comparison with the precious pearl—and *sponges.*

Among other creatures of the sea

 The Shark should be described;

among plants,

 The Sugar-cane;[1]

and from the mineral kingdom *gold*, upon the acquisition of which the Spaniards directed all their force; or this can be reserved till the conquest of Mexico.

b. Physics.

Columbus took as his guide at sea the mariner's compass. Description of it.

A sewing needle should be magnetized and balanced, when it will, like the needle of the compass, point to the north. This circumstance, in connection with the fact, that the compass needle during Columbus's first voyage pointed towards the west, introduces the subject of earth magnetism. Magnetism must be treated in some detail at this point (electro-magnetism).

The descriptions of the treasures of the sea lead to the question how they reach daylight, and thus to the description of

 Divers.

Experiments and apparatus generally;
The diving-bell, and swimming.

c. Chemistry.

If gold be described, the difference between precious and base metals must be pointed out. This leads to the oxidizing of iron and copper.

The possibility of breathing in the diving-bell and the necessity of the conveyance of fresh air thereto, point to the elements of the air (oxygen).

---

[1] The tobacco and potato plants can also be taken here unless, in consideration of the large amount of material available, they are reserved till their introduction into Eng and is given.

ARITHMETIC.

Arithmetic at this stage has to teach *fractions*. The nature of fractions may be illustrated by making a compass card. The line from north to south divides the compass in halves, the line from east to west in quarters. The next subdivision gives eighths, the next sixteenths, and the last thirty-seconds, with which the usual division of the compass ends. The nature of proper and improper, simple and mixed fractions, reduction of fractions, may be demonstrated by means of it. For the two last operations the division of the compass into degrees is particularly useful. A further exercise would be the division of a circular grass-plot or garden-bed.

Decimal fractions should be taught as the complements of whole numbers, from one backwards. They can, however, be taught in connection with vulgar fractions.

The amount of alloy in gold supplies arithmetical matter for ordinary calculations in fractions. Further, we may reckon, for example, what proportion of the entire population of Cuba are (*a*) white; (*b*) coloured; (*c*) Asiatic; (*d*) negroes. In using decimal fractions, the rate per cent. must be found. Again, we can exercise vulgar as well as decimal fractions in calculating the receipts, expenditure, debts, imports and exports, of the West India Islands, the relation between supply and demand in those islands, the proportion of tobacco produced in Germany and Cuba, and the postal and telegraph service with the West Indies and North American States.[1] It cannot be denied that a careful collection of statistics is necessary, if we are to obtain matter for arithmetic lessons from lessons on objects. Handbooks of geography and the encyclopædia, however, contain much of the necessary material. In the business advertisements of every newspaper, we can find arithmetical examples from practical life.

---

[1] The necessary numbers can be taken from the tariff, which may be obtained at any post-office.

The suggestions for the following subjects are made by Ufer, though they have not yet been practically applied by him:—

GEOMETRY.

With the compass lessons, lessons on the circle may be connected. The lines which mark the direction of the heavens are radii forming the diameter. The declination of the needle leads to the division of the circle into degrees, and this again to the measurement of angles by degrees. Then follow lessons on the ellipse and the oval, and comparison of them with the circle. The measurement of the circle may follow later, and in connection with a concrete example—for instance, the measurement of a circular grass-plot.

DRAWING.

Figures (ornamental) are drawn consisting of circles, ellipses, ovals, or their parts. They may be found in any large work on drawing.

Experiments remain to be made, whether the forms of sea-life (shells, star-fish, sea nettles) or tropical plants are suitable as drawing copies for this stage, and, again, whether some material can be taken from the history of the development of art.

SINGING.

(Here also English material similar to the German is substituted for it.)

There is a wealth of material for use in singing. There are religious songs connected with the life of Jesus, and many devout moments in the life of Columbus which can be concentrated in a hymn.

Before starting on his voyage he prayed. This may suggest Charles Wesley's two hymns,

"God of my life, whose gracious power,"

and

"Forth in Thy name, O Lord, I go."

When he landed, he returned thanks to God. Connected hymn,

"Now thank we all our God."

To the life of Columbus as a whole the hymns apply,
"The Lord my pasture shall prepare,"
and
"Jesus, Lover of my soul,"
and Whittier's hymn embodies the lesson of his death,
"God calls our loved ones, but we lose not wholly
What He has given;
They live on earth in thought and deed, as truly
As in His heaven."

To many it will appear strange, that religious songs should be sung in connection with secular subjects. It must be remembered that occurrences similar to those in the life of Columbus are to be found in the child's life, and expressed in song.

Maritime songs may be introduced: "Rule, Britannia," "Ye Mariners of England," "Tom Bowling," and "Toll for the Brave." Any difficulties in the text of these may be introduced and explained in the lesson on English.

FRENCH.

The *Atala* of Chateaubriand should be read, or *Paul and Virginia*, by Bernardin de St. Pierre. The grammar must be connected with the readings.

The assertion made by the adherents of the dual theory, that *connecting points* only are made between the different branches, seems to make it clear, that they do not aim at any *systematic* connection between the subjects of the curriculum. All that appears to be implied is, that problems, facts, examples, suggestions, can be taken from the concentration subjects for the rest, and apperception is strengthened thereby. For instance in the series just illustrated, the seaweed would be described under botany, and the compass is used in arithmetic to illustrate fractions and decimals.

The following English material has been suggested to follow the first and second culture epochs (fairy tales and *Robinson Crusoe*), which would remain the same for English schools, and to run parallel to the concentration centres of Ziller: third year, *Old English Legends*, characteristic of the earliest days, which may be chosen without a strict regard to chronology; they would, above all, include the legends of King Arthur and the Round Table, Robin Hood, etc.: fourth and fifth years, *The Settlement of England*, as presented in its legends (see Freeman's *Old English History*), *The Anglo-Saxon Forefathers*, *The Danes*, and *The Christianization of England* (Egbert, Alfred, Canute, Augustine, Paulinus, Dunstan, etc.): sixth year, *Great English Kings from William the Conqueror to the Wars of the Roses*: seventh year, *Renaissance, Reformation, Age of Discovery to 1763*: eighth year, *Development of Modern England*.[1]

The reader can now to some extent judge for himself whether, as Prof. Rein and the adherents of the dual theory maintain, the connection between the material of the different subjects can be so kept up as to form true apperception, or whether, as Voigt and its opponents contend, the connection is so weak that any real apperception is impossible.

---

[1] Quoted from Rein's *Outlines of Pedagogics*, translated by C. and T. van Liew.

CHAPTER IV

MORAL STRENGTH OF CHARACTER; GOVERNMENT AND DISCIPLINE

Section I.—Government

Insight alone insufficient to form the will. Educative instruction has so to form the circle of thought, that from it will proceeds. Willing presumes, as we have already seen, a certain degree of insight; without insight there is no will. But it presumes more. With insight, interest, which in Herbart's psychology is the root of will, must be combined. The aim of an educative instruction is thus to create an insight which impels the will to do what it ought.

From insight, the pupil must learn whether the aim and means of his action are morally commendable. If instruction has created an insight in accordance with the moral ideas, which impels to will, its aim is accomplished, but by no means the aim of education. If the latter stopped at this point, it would form cultivated men whose morality would teach them what to do and leave undone, men who ardently desired good and condemned evil, but yet whose will and insight might not be in harmony with each other, when obedience to the moral involved difficulties and self-sacrifice. The actions of such men would be almost entirely determined by circumstances, and with them their volitions would change. The very nature of their will would be variable, as, although the moral insight might be perfect, the will to act upon it might be infirm; none could predict what in a given case their actions would be. On such characters no reliance could be placed; they would be, and often are, bending reeds, moved hither and thither by chance winds.

Discipline used in the direct formation of character. Hence it follows, that another educative activity is required, if willing in its entirety is to be always in harmony with the moral ideas. This influence is *discipline*,[1] culture in a narrower sense, or *direct formation of character*. The teacher using it seeks to strengthen right willing, on the basis of a right insight gained by instruction. Thus it follows, discipline can only accomplish its work, when and in so far as the teacher has done the work of instruction successfully, *i.e.*, created moral insight. Discipline, therefore, commences later than the beginning of instruction, and moves with it side by side. Before the child, however, has gained insight, his actions must be under control; he must be punctual, quiet, cleanly, orderly, diligent. When he transgresses in such matters, his intention is not evil; hence these faults are not morally blamable. But they are disturbing, and hinder the teacher's work; they injure others, often the child himself, and if not checked, form the fruitful germs of bad habits. What the child is to do and leave undone *before he attains to insight*, belongs to *government*.

There are thus in Herbart's system of education three educational activities: *government*, *instruction*, and *discipline*. Instruction has already been treated of under the head of practical pedagogy; we pass on now to government.

The aim of government. Its aim is not to form character, but to keep order, to check everything which, though not

---

[1] The term *Zucht*, translated here and in the *Science of Education* by *discipline*, is used by Herbart to signify that part of education, the aim of which is *direct formation of character*. It must not be confounded with the term *discipline*, or *Zucht*, when used by other German writers, notably by Kant, as the exact equivalent of that part of education called by Herbart government (*Regierung*), the aim of which is *to maintain order*, and thereby prepare the way for the work of instruction and discipline. As a rendering of *Zucht*, *discipline*, as the term is *used in England*, appears to be a better rendering of Herbart's than the alternative one: training. A well-disciplined character suggests that personal activity of the pupil in the process of its formation which was to Herbart an indispensable, indeed, the most important factor; while a well-trained character suggests the teacher, or some other external influence only as its maker.

intentional, and therefore not intrinsically bad, disturbs the work of instruction and discipline, troubles parents and teachers, or harms them and the child himself Herbart calls it "the requisite presumption of education; it has no aim to attain in the child's disposition, except to create a spirit of order."[1] "It works for the present, and thereby differs from both instruction and discipline, which both work for future culture."[2]

Measures employed by government: first, occupation. The measures employed by teachers and parents for the government of children, are comprised under four heads. *Occupation.*—"The basis of all government is occupation."[3] Here another distinction between government and instruction is apparent. "In instruction, what is to be taught and learned must in no wise be left to chance; in government, *what* is learned is indifferent so long as naughtiness be subdued."[4] The great object is not that the child shall gain mentally, but that his time shall be occupied. "Self-chosen occupations are the best, but the child must be helped to follow them out regularly and consecutively, so that they do not degenerate into mere aimless play, of which he soon wearies. It is very desirable that adults who have sufficient patience, should join in children's games (which are an important part of occupation), explain pictures, and tell them stories."[5]

One of the most important parts of occupation is play. It keeps the child from idleness and all its attendant evils, and checks the growth of harmful habits which have their root in it.

Second, supervision. *Supervision* —Herbart's opinion about strict supervision is clearly and emphatically given in the *Science of Education.* The evils of it are, it leads directly to deceitful efforts to escape it, because it is so burdensome; the need for it grows with use; it stifles originality; it prevents children from winning that self-knowledge which can only be obtained in free self-activity; in a word,

---

[1] *Umriss pädagogischer Vorlesungen,* 44.   [2] *Ibid.,* 57.   [3] *Ibid.,* 46.
[4] *Ibid.,* 61.   [5] *Ibid.,* 47.

it defeats the very end of all education: the formation of character. "Those who grow up merely passive as obedient children, have no character when they are released from supervision. The old pedagogy betrayed its weakness in nothing so much as its dependence upon compulsion, the modern in nothing so much as the emphatic value it places upon supervision." On this point Herbart and Rousseau are in accord. "Let the child," says Rousseau, "run about, play, fall down a hundred times a day, the oftener the better, as he will the sooner learn to get up again by himself. The boon of freedom is worth many scars. You will make a mere animal of him, if you are continually directing him." The mere presence of a teacher, if he be loved and respected, is, according to Herbart, sufficient to keep children in due bounds and make severer measures unnecessary.

Third and fourth: threatening and punishment.

Threatening and punishment.—In these measures of government, an essential difference between its procedures and those of discipline becomes apparent. Bad action, "the intention, so far as it becomes, or could become, act, is," says Herbart, "to be richly punished." "Of the bad will," by which it is only *apparently* prompted, "the teacher at this stage must take no notice," for the reason that *will* in the true sense does not yet exist in the child. The correction of the bad will—in Herbart's words, "wounding the desire to do evil"[1]—is reserved for the punishments of discipline, when moral insight has to some extent been formed, and the child can at least partially recognise the goodness of the teacher's will, and the justice of the punishments he inflicts. Because insight is not possible to the little child, Rousseau would abolish punishments of every kind entirely. "Inflict upon the child no kind of punishment; . . . his actions being without moral quality, he can do nothing morally bad, or which deserves punishment or reproof."[2] Herbart, on the contrary, *would* inflict punishments, not directed upon the will, which he sees with Rousseau does not exist, but simply to subdue what

---

[1] *Science of Education*, p. 99.   [2] *Émile*, Rousseau, Book III.

he calls "the principle of disorder, the wild impetuosity,"[1] which at present occupies the place of the true will, and with the sole object of *establishing the habit of obedience*. Obedience is of two kinds. Either the child obeys the teacher's will without knowing his reasons, or this will is carried out when the pupil has made it his own, after due consideration. The latter is the obedience created and appealed to by discipline; the former is the obedience established by government — in Herbart's words, "blind obedience," "passive obedience to authority." The former, "obedience which can be associated with the child's own will, is only to be expected as the result of a somewhat advanced stage of genuine education."[2]

Reasoning with little children. As a natural corollary of the preceding, Herbart, unlike Locke, and like Rousseau, condemns the habit of reasoning with the child who is still under government. "The tone of government, unlike that of discipline," is short and sharp; "the child submits to it because he must."[3] Its object is not to form character, but to inspire awe. Neither reasons nor explanations ought to be given; all punishments should be enforced, without pointing out to the child the naughtiness of the mischief done, without exciting his mind. They must be to him as a natural, necessary consequence by which he will be trained and made wise. Locke, on the contrary, not only considered children should be reasoned with, but also that they were capable of it, and it should be begun with them, as soon as they could speak: "I cannot but think that reasoning is the true way of dealing with children. They understand it as early as they do language."[4] This and his idea that the love of credit and fear of shame and disgrace can be appealed to in little children,[5] seem to have originated in a common error, *i.e.*, that intellectual power and moral insight are already considerably developed in the child. "It is labour lost," says Kant, "to speak of duty to children. One ought not to try to call

---

[1] *Science of Education*, p. 95.   [2] *Ibid.*, p. 102.   [3] *Ibid.*, p. 234.
[4] *Thoughts on Education*, Locke (Pitt Series), p. 60.   [5] *Ibid.*, p. 84.

into play with children the fear of shame, but to wait for this, till the period of youth comes. In fact, it cannot be developed in them till the idea of honour has already taken root there." Rousseau declares, like Herbart, the impossibility of reasoning with children: "I find nothing more stupid than children who have been so much reasoned with. Reason, apparently a compound of all other faculties, the one latest developed and with the most difficulty, is the one proposed as agent in unfolding the faculties earliest used! The noblest work of education is to make a reasoning man, and we expect to train a young child by making him reason! This is beginning at the end; this is making an instrument of a result. I would rather require a child ten years old to be five feet tall, than to be judicious." [1]

Herbart's view of corporal punishment. Herbart's expression "threats in case of need enforced by compulsion," [2] as used by government, suggests the question, What was his opinion in regard to corporal punishment? Not that of Locke: "The rod is a slavish discipline, which makes a slavish temper; there is one, and but one, fault for which I think children should be beaten, and that is obstinacy or rebellion." [3] Nor was it that of Rousseau, who, as before mentioned, would "inflict no punishment whatever." "Corporal punishments" (here used in the wide sense of chastisement, confinement, deprivation of food, etc.), says Herbart, "which come in when reproof is unavailing, cannot be entirely dispensed with. But they ought to be so rare, that they are feared rather as something impending than as actually carried into effect." Above all, he points out, they are to be carefully regulated by, and adapted to, the age and stage of the pupil's development: "It does not hurt the boy to remember he sometimes had the rod when a child. Again, it does not hurt him if he places the impossibility of his now having the rod on the same level as the impossibility that he could deserve it. But such a severe wound to his sense of honour would certainly be hurtful to him, if he already thought

---

[1] Émile, Rousseau, p. 52. [2] Science of Education, p. 102.
[3] Thoughts on Education, Locke, pp. 30, 56.

little of bodily pain; and in the highest degree it becomes harmful when children, already hardened by beating, receive more. The greatest callousness is its result, and we can hardly hope that long care, now become indispensable, will bring back natural feeling." [1]

Authority and love to guide the measures of government. The means by which these measures of government are to be regulated and used are, says Herbart, authority and love: an authority which must "depend on superiority of mind" [2]; a love which "must never degenerate into undue indulgence." "That authority and love secure government better than any harsher means, is well known. Kindness stops just at the point where government is most necessary, and love must never be purchased by weak indulgence. It is only of value when combined with the necessary severity." [3] Since "nature has entrusted these means of government—authority and love—to the parents, it is best left in their hands." If however it passes into the hands of others, it should be carried on with as little friction as possible, and the amount of this, adds Herbart as a warning, depends on the proportion which the children's activity bears to the amount of free play they get.

The teacher who has authority and the children's love, easily wins their obedience. "The mind instinctively bends to authority. When children are healthy," says Herbart, "government in early life is comparatively simple, and, once tractableness is formed, can be easily carried on. But it must not be interrupted. If children are only left to themselves or strangers for a few days, the difference is apparent; it costs trouble to adjust the reins, and this must not be done suddenly." [4] Hence he lays much stress upon the value of "that strict regularity of daily life, which some parents carefully provide for through their household arrangements. This, however, must never become so painfully strict, that it unduly represses children's natural energy." [5]

When government has been successful, the pupil has learned

---

[1] *Umriss pädagogischer Vorlesungen*, 51.   [2] *Science of Education*, p. 99.
[3] *Umriss pädagogischer Vorlesungen*, 53.   [4] *Ibid.*, 54.
[5] *Science of Education*, p. 218.

obedience; moreover, he has unconsciously become habituated to order, cleanliness, diligence, punctuality, etc. Government has thereby prepared the ground in the child's soul, upon which instruction and discipline are to work in the future.

Section II.—Discipline

The aim of discipline. We come now to the third division of education— *discipline*—which deserves the teacher's most careful attention and thought, for it deals with nothing less than the *moral foundation of character*, the method by which the circle of thought may be brought to generate the good will.

Contrast of discipline with government. If we contrast discipline with government, the essential differences in their natures and functions become apparent. It is these differences which, although discipline and government sometimes use the same measures, determine, in Herbart's words, the "distinctions in their *mode* of use."[1]

To government the child submits because he *must*, to discipline because he *wills* to do so. "Discipline finds room only so far as an inward experience persuades its pupil to submit to it willingly; its power only reaches so far as the pupil's assent meets it." The tone of government is "short and sharp; that of discipline is continuous, persevering, slowly penetrating, only ceasing by degrees." Government "subdues by force"; "discipline is a moulding power which animates while it constrains, but follows there, and there only, its natural direction when it directly encourages and attracts."[2] As regards the punishments of government, "the teacher must guard against mingling with them any of that personal influence acting on the mind, which ought to remain in reserve for the punishments of discipline alone; in the punishments of discipline, the teacher's personal influence is, as hereafter shown, all-important." The punishments of government merely "render the deserved quantum of good or ill, no matter in what way"; "those of discipline avoid the positive and arbitrary as much as possible, and it lays hold, when it can, solely of the natural

---

[1] *Science of Education*, p. 229. [2] *Ibid.*, p. 234.

consequences of actions." "He who wastes his time must lose pleasure; he who spoils his things must be deprived of them; he who eats too much must have bitter medicine; he who chatters, be sent away."¹ As to the nature of reward, Herbart writes, "Spoiling by continuous unnecessary pleasure, by artificially produced enjoyments, connected neither with work nor training, is harmful, because the blunting of sensibility which results therefrom, deprives discipline of many minor aids which it can profitably use with children. Little is needed to give pleasure in a variety of ways, when temperateness is the habit of daily life"² The punishments of government "are *bound* to a proportionate retribution; those of discipline are preferably not so. The latter must only be so meted out that they always appear to the individual as well-meant warnings, and do not excite lasting opposition to the teacher."³ Government must disappear sooner than discipline; the teacher who "uses the same act with older, that served him well with younger, children," who continues to govern when the pupil is sufficiently developed to be disciplined, "produces a strained relationship, which continues intolerable and irremediable during the whole future."⁴

Discipline must help to form a moral will.
The work of discipline is to ensure that the pupil shall not only during the period of education, but also afterwards, *will* only what can stand before the moral judgment, and not will what is opposed to it. Its effort then must be "that the willing of the pupil shall receive a direction determined by the moral ideas, that every later act of volition shall carry the impress of a personality, which has placed its will entirely in the service of those moral ideas."

The principle of apperception applied to formation of will.
To understand the way by which such a direction may be given, the nature of willing must be understood. Willing, as already noticed, grows out of desire, when with the latter its attainment seems possible. Thus reflection, occupied with the difficulties, duties,

---

¹ *Umriss pädagogischer Vorlesungen*, 157.   ² *Ibid.*, 157.
³ *Science of Education*, p. 243.   ⁴ *Ibid.*, p. 229.

motives, etc. involved, precedes willing. Consequently, with every act of willing, a large number of presentations are simultaneously raised into consciousness, by what has been previously termed active reproduction.[1] In consequence of this reproduction, the presentations in question assume a united character. With the attainment of what is willed, pleasure is combined; a picture of the act of willing remains in the mind, in which an impulse dwells to become as clear as possible, to realize itself, *i.e.*, to reproduce that feeling of pleasure which made itself felt at the first willing. Such a will-picture created by a single instance is called "single volition" (*Einzelwollung*). The oftener, then, precisely the same act of willing is repeated, the stronger will be the "single volition." The connection between this fact and the law that identical presentations coalesce to form a single clear presentation, is obvious.[2] Ultimately, by the fusion of these acts of willing with the single volition, a definite habit of willing is formed, a habit which, if fostered long enough, cannot be given up.

Let us suppose that such a will-picture is formed in the mind, and that a new willing similar to, *not identical with*, the former arises from the circle of thought. Then, in obedience to the law of similarity, the presentations determining the first willing are set in motion, and simultaneously the will-picture then acquired rises into consciousness. This will-picture strives to attain clearness, examines the new willing, finds that it lies in the same direction as itself, and that through its realization, the impulse dwelling in the older will-picture will, on the whole, be satisfied. Thus the new willing, strengthened by the old picture, is much more energetically realized than it would otherwise be. Two analogous will-pictures now exist, which operate on each other in the same way as analogous presentations.[3] As with the latter, identical elements combine to form ultimately a psychic or logical concept, so the identical elements in the individual acts of willing attract each other

---

[1] See p. 29. [2] See p. 23.
[3] See p. 23. For the sake of clearness, we think of the will-pictures, to begin with, as apart; in reality their combination takes place during the act of willing.

mutually. They repel all that is disparate and contradictory in the presentations wherein they originate, and melt into a new will-picture, which is not only stronger and more vivid, but also purer, since it is kept free from the individual peculiarities of the single volition. Herbart refers to this fact—that the laws which govern the mutual action of presentations govern also the formation of will—in these words: "I am astonished that a parallel has not been more carefully drawn between the constancy of our conceptions and the constancy of willing, which goes to make up the chief basis of the objective part of character."[1] The single volition has now grown into a more general will, which may be compared with the psychic concept. Like the psychic concept, which is made more general, and approaches the logical concept by additional perceptions, this more general will becomes with each new similar willing, yet more general, until out of the fusions of single willings *the will* is formed. The effect of previous will-pictures, both good and bad, upon present willing is finely estimated by one of our greatest English prose poets in the following words: "Our lives make a moral tradition for our individual selves, as the life of mankind at large makes a moral tradition for the race, and to have once acted greatly seems a reason why we should always be noble. But Tito was feeling the effect of an opposite tradition: he had won no memories of self-conquest and perfect faithfulness from which he could have a sense of falling."[2]

Action of disparate presentations in the formation of will.
Up to this point we have assumed that the single willings have been met by a will similar in nature to themselves. What would be the psychical process were they met by a will *opposed* to themselves? Perhaps the already-acquired will-picture would be reproduced by the law of contrast, and the former, finding that the new willing was at variance with itself, and thus that the clearness after which it was striving was checked by it, would suppress the new willing. If however every act of volition were not suppressed which was entirely at variance with the already-acquired will-picture, either the latter would be wanting

---

[1] *Science of Education*, p. 202. [2] *Romola*, chap. xxxix.

in essential force, or it would be entirely unreproduced; in other words, memory of the will would be weak or altogether gone.

Memory of the will: its conditions. *Memory of the will* (reproduction of the will-picture) depends, as we have seen, on the movement of the presentations in whose interactions the will-picture originated. Herbart terms it "the primary requisite of character," and shows that "it stands in closest connection with the degree of the mind's mobility. The slow-minded, those who live in their own world, hold, pursue, cultivate their own objects, are difficult to move from their track, and often appear stubborn and stupid, without being either the one or the other; these, if they are clear-minded also, possess the healthy will, which when once won, affords education a firm footing, because in them memory of the will is strongest." If the will-picture is to be clear and vigorous, the presentations must be closely combined. This is the case after energetic and matured reflection; an act of will which has cost us that can be recalled vividly to memory. Further, the whole circle of thought must be so interconnected that the presentations essential to the will at any moment are immediately set in motion, in order that the influence of the will-picture on the new willing is not too late in its operation, and does not first put in its appearance when the new willing has already passed into action. In the latter case the old will-picture encounters a new one, finished and unlike itself, the results of the encounter being, that the old will is checked in its effort after clearness, and a feeling of pain (remorse) is caused thereby. When memory of the will is strong, and action so rapid, that apperception between the cumulative will and the single willing takes place unconsciously, it becomes "the inexorable law of human souls, that we prepare ourselves for sudden deeds, by the reiterated choice of good or evil, that gradually determines character."[1] Memory of will then depends on the firm union and systematic order of the presentations. The influence which instruction exercises over memory of the will becomes very obvious at this point, and its

---

[1] *Romola*, George Eliot, p. 205.

effect on the entire culture of the Will, will be still more apparent later on.

Conditions and results of will apperception. The older cumulative will examines and tests the new—the potential act of will—thus: The two series of presentations which form the basis of the cumulative will and the potential act of will face each other, as it were, a while, and the older and stronger series, that in which the cumulative will resides, examines whether in the more recent, weaker, potential volition, there are sufficient elements similar to its own, for a fusion of the two masses of thought to take place. If not, and they are opposed to each other in many essential elements, the single act cannot be apperceived by the cumulative will, and the latter repels the former as untenable. In common parlance, we abandon our resolution because "second thoughts are best," or because "on reflection we look at the thing differently." If, on the other hand, the single willing and the cumulative will are harmonious, a fusion, *an apperception, takes place*. The masses of thought thus united reach a totality of effort far exceeding that which the single willing could have attained. The latter gains a high degree of energy and power of resistance, while the cumulative will is strengthened by the single willing newly apperceived.

Maxims: Herbart's employment of the term. The examination of the new presentation series by the old as to the suitability of the former for being apperceived, calls forth a judgment, whether the single willing is or is not harmonious with the cumulative will. Since the cumulative will strives to attain clearness with this judgment, a command or a prohibition to the new act of will is combined with it. This combination of judgment and command, when it applies not merely to a single instance, but to a class of many such, is called a *principle* or *maxim*.

He who is taught when young to feed the hungry, gains in time a cumulative will directed to the aid of all in need. Every single willing which harmonizes with the cumulative will is strengthened; every one opposing it is repelled. A general judgment is formed, which on every occasion comes forth as a prohibition or command. This judgment (practical principle, maxim) is "Help thy neighbour in his need." As it applied to all previous cognate cases, it supplies a norm for every future act of will of the same class. If it rises to a psychic force, the future existence of an entire class of volitions in harmony with morality, is secured.

If an ethical principle is to become a psychical power and rule the single willings through its apperceiving force, it must not be merely commanded, learned. If it is to rule the life, it must be rooted in and through life, for true maxims are nothing more nor less than part of a man's experience in life. Maxims originating in reflection (as, for instance, in instruction) must be *lived*, if they are to become real. Their constant use must develop a habit founded on insight which cannot be given up.

The subjective part of character, the growth of later years. Discipline must *lead* the pupil to place all classes of volition under the rule of living moral maxims, if a "calm great passion for the good" is to be created. But it must be carefully noted that maxims, principles, etc., belong to the subjective side of character, and this is mainly formed during the later years of education; when the teacher is leading the pupil, under the guidance of discipline, through " a making he himself discovers when choosing the good and rejecting the bad, to form his own character." A lifetime indeed is insufficient to build up the subjective side of character, to reach the ideal of morality. The teacher can only prepare the basis of it, and direct and regulate its early growth by discipline. "The stamping in of maxims," says Herbart, "on little children, even when everything goes as well as possible, unduly hastens and disturbs the subjective formation of character, besides being harmful to childlike ingenuousness."

The objective side of character the earlier growth. It is to the "objective part of character, that which forms and raises itself slowly enough under the influence of education, to which the teacher must at first devote his chief attention."[1] For to

---

[1] *Science of Education*, p. 202.

it belong the whole of the child's inclinations and desires, which will be presented to the judgment, to be sanctioned and raised into principles by the subjective, during the later years of education and the rest of life. These desires must be regulated and corrected; the teacher must check and eradicate some, generate, encourage, and strengthen others, using for that purpose the wealth of many-sided interest provided by instruction, and doing it by the constraining, attractive power of discipline. When the formation of the objective does not precede that of the subjective, and the desires are allowed to develop under the mere external constraint of regulating maxims, the boy will probably afterwards form his maxims to suit his inclinations, that he may enjoy the inward prescriptive right to do as he pleases. For the subjective readily finds principles answering to the inclinations. The man who is mean in little things will justify himself by the maxim, "Take care of the pence; the pounds will take care of themselves." "If the objective side—the desires—be bad, and the subjective does not sanction them—that is, if the latter be morally pure, so that the judgment it passes on the self is as impartial as that it would pass on a stranger"[1]—the two sides of character are not in harmony, and "those which combined would have strengthened it, now chafe and disintegrate it."[2] If the desires are bad, and the subjective sanctions them, the character is immoral; if they are good, and recognized to be such by the subjective—"if they pass into the subjective of the character, and express themselves as principles[3]—the will takes law, the principle of order, and the objects of its endeavours, from what the intuitive judgment has marked with unqualified approval or disapproval."[4] The character is moral because the desires are placed in the service of the moral ideas.

Desires and their regulation by discipline. Herbart confronts the entire sphere of desire, which is determinable, with the practical ideas of rectitude (right and equity),[5] goodness, and inner freedom, by which it is determined. The

[1] *Science of Education*, p. 204.   [2] *Ibid.*, p. 201.   [3] *Ibid.*, p. 208.
[4] *Ibid.*, p. 261.   [5] See pp. 70, 72.

two ideas of right and equity he combines in the *Science of Education* in one idea : that of rectitude. The reason for this combination in education of diverse ideas is, he explains, " because there they are generally created contemporaneously and by the same circumstances; they enter into the same decisions, and therefore it is not easy to suppose that an ingenuous mind, which makes its moral insight more keen for the one, will not at the same time do so for the other."[1] The practical application of the twofold idea of rectitude is shown in the following passage : " We may lay it down as a principle never to disturb what exists among children " (*i.e.*, any law they may make for themselves based on the idea of right) " without good reason " (*i.e.*, a grave infringement of the idea of equity). " When disputes arise, we must first ascertain what has been settled and agreed upon amongst the children themselves " (idea of right), " and must take the part of the one who in any sort of way has been deprived of his own." Then we must try to help " each one to what he deserves," (idea of equity) " so far as this is possible, without violent injury to justice."[2] Herbart shows even amongst a children's community the working of one of his sociological ideas : that of an administrative system, derived from the idea of benevolence,[3] where each member of society must contribute as much as possible to the welfare of the whole, that the State may be prosperous and well administered. With children this idea of an administrative system must be so used, " that we point beyond the idea of rectitude to what is best for the common good, as that to which it is right both property and merit shall be spontaneously sacrificed, and which will be for all the chief measure for future agreements."[4]

With regard to the cultivation of the idea of rectitude in children, Herbart says, " When we want to cultivate the sense of right in children, we must carefully distinguish the relationship of right which exists between children and adults, from that which exists between children themselves. In the former

---

[1] *Science of Education*, p. 260.   [2] *Ibid.*, p. 261.   [3] See p. 74.
[4] *Science of Education*, p. 261.

we should give or entrust something under conditions, or give over anything that is harmless, entirely to their own control. For example, we ought not to complain when the boy plucks a flower which has been given him, or leaves his *own* piece of garden uncultivated. If children establish relationships of right among *themselves*, however, we ought to show and defend the highest aspect of the idea. If a boy takes his stand on his 'rights' to the detriment of 'benevolence,' the teacher can easily put him out of conceit of the 'rights,' or, better still, can be more sparing of his favours, which the boy cannot demand as a right. Children desist from their rights only too readily, when they think they are obliged to obey; another time when this compulsion is not present, they will take good care not to do so. It is very difficult to make the child desist 'benevolently' from his rights. Like the authority of great despots over little despots in a country, parents exercise a kind of sovereignty over their children's property. It obscures the conception of contract and right to meddle with things already given, or to threaten that if the child spoils them, they will be taken away. Instead of this, from the earliest years the idea of right in many aspects should be engraven on the child's innermost soul, so that he may learn to consider the rights of others sacred. It is of supreme importance in life." [1]

For the purposes of education, Herbart divides the desires, which he confronts in their entirety with these three practical ideas, into three groups: (1) those directed to what an individual chooses to endure; (2) to what he wishes to possess; (3) to what he wishes to do. Under the guidance of discipline, the first class in the child will be regulated by "exercises in patience," the second by "exercises in acquisitiveness," the third by "exercises in industry." [2] Of the last, play, which the teacher has watched, and in which he takes part with an understanding sympathy, forms an important part. " We may always play with the child, guide him in playing to something useful, if we have previously understood the earnestness which lies in his play, and the spontaneous efforts with which

---

[1] *Aphorismen zur Pädagogik.*   [2] *Science of Education*, p. 257.

he will work himself out in happy moments, and also if we know how to abstain from such condescension as would check his upward efforts, for in such upward efforts in the childish things, which will soon be left behind, he would have received instruction." [1]

The personality of the teacher. With Locke and Rousseau,[2] Herbart attaches immense importance to the personality of the teacher: to the superiority of mind by which he obtains authority: to the love which never stoops, except to raise the child; to the discernment which will recognize the existent good in the child, and the nobility which will raise him by making it valuable in his eyes; to the equableness of behaviour, the consistency and justice of treatment, which will help to preserve and increase in the child that all-important factor in the formation of character, memory of the will. On the personality of the teacher greatly depend the force and efficacy of approbation and blame, most important measures of discipline in Herbart's system.

Approbation and blame. Herbart has happily called giving joy by deserved approbation "*the fine art of discipline.*" He carefully distinguishes it from praise, which he considers "mostly poisonous to the young, making them proud and regardful of words rather than love." Discipline, he points out, can never have its full force, till after it has found an opportunity of showing to the pupil his better self, by means of an approbation powerfully affecting him. In words of earnest warning, which both the too indulgent and too strict teacher may alike take to heart, Herbart repeatedly shows, that until this better self has been discerned by both teacher and pupil, blame can have no effect. "Reproof," says he, "falls on receptive ears, only when it has ceased to stand alone as a minus quantity; it must only threaten to cancel an approbation

---

[1] *Science of Education*, p. 257.
[2] "The tutor's example must lead the child into what he would have him do. His practice must by no means cross his precepts, unless he intends to set him wrong" (*Thoughts on Education*, Locke). "Remember that before you venture an undertaking to form a man, you must have made yourself a man; you must find in yourself the example you ought to offer to him" (*Émile*, Rousseau).

already won, for those alone feel the stress of inward reproaches who have attained to self-respect, and fear to lose something of it."[1]

Genesis of objective and subjective character in children. Children have at first no character; only by degrees is one formed in their circle of thought. What they do or leave undone, keep or give up, suffer or refuse to suffer, is not regulated by moral principles. The commencement of this subordination to principles is simultaneous with the commencement of isolated general volitions, which have been formed out of several similar acts of will. These general volitions are the centres of crystallization in the fluid element of single willings, by which the latter are attracted and *apperceived*, if their nature admit of it. These general volitions, which determine— that is to say, apperceive or suppress—the single willings, form the beginning of what Herbart calls the *subjective* part of character. This consists of the will based on the intuitive judgments formed by the apperceiving masses of presentations. Opposite to it is what we have seen to be an earlier growth, the *objective* part, *i.e.*, the single willings growing out of manifold desires. The subjective, as Herbart repeatedly proves, is the determining, the objective the determined, part of character.

The joint work of instruction and discipline on character. The extreme importance of instruction for the objective side of character, may be gathered from what has been already said on the nature of interest. The aim of instruction is to arouse many-sided interest, out of which grows a many-sided volition, and discipline "must form the frame of mind which makes such instruction possible."[2] In regard to the subjective side of character, the task common to both discipline and instruction is: first, to guard against the formation near or after each other of several ruling circles of thought: second, to ensure *that* unity of the ruling circle upon which memory of the will, the energy and sequence of volition peculiar to character, rests, which, forming a protection against the storms of passion,

---

[1] *Science of Education*, p. 238.   [2] *Ibid.*, p. 238.

when combined with insight makes a man truly free. "Nothing is more evident," says Herbart, "than that the passionate man is a slave; his incapacity to consider motives of duty or advantage, his ruin through his own fault, are clearly evident. In contrast with him, the reasoning man, who represses his desires as soon as they are opposed by considerations of good, may rightly be called free, and the stronger he is in this power of repression, the freer he is." [1]

The relation of discipline to interest. "Direct formation of character" (discipline), says Ziller, "must place the pupil in a position, and open up to his interest opportunities, where he can turn his thoughts into action on the lines of that interest."

These opportunities must not however be so numerous that memory of the will, which it is "the work of discipline to complete," suffers. Memory of the will, it will be remembered, can only be formed when similar acts of will are often repeated. Hence the teacher ought to cultivate the child's will by discipline "in the midst of a simple uniform mode of life, and the absence of all disturbing change." [2]

In strictly ordered life, "where right," says Goethe, "is not regarded as medicine, but as daily diet," steady, regularly recurring acts are possible, from which not desultory single willings, but the will of the individual, can be formed through the power of apperception. To this end, every willing must be in accord with memory; that is to say, it must be such that there is no need to consider what its expression in action is to be, because that is in every case determined beforehand. "A man," says Herbart, "whose will does not spontaneously reappear as *the same* as often as the occasion recurs, a man who is obliged to carry himself back by reflection to his former resolution, will have great trouble in building up his character. It is because natural constancy of will is not often found in children, that discipline has so much to do." [3]

Measures of discipline. Discipline must restrain, determine, regulate. Where there is no memory of the will, and its place is filled by caprice, discipline must both compel

---

[1] *Lehrbuch zur Psychologie*, 119.   [2] *Science of Education*, p. 242.
[3] *Ibid.*, p. 203.

and restrain the pupil, that his will may grow united and harmonious. Discipline must also work determiningly. It must teach the pupil himself to choose, not the teacher in the name of the pupil, for the pupil's is the character to be determined. When the subjective side of character begins to form, regulating discipline comes in. While reasoning should, according to Herbart, never be used with a child, directly the pupil can begin to reason, he should not be left entirely to himself. The teacher must enter into his thoughts and difficulties, and guard against their taking a wrong direction. Finally, even if the pupil has reached the stage of moral resolution, he must through discipline, " by frequent reminders and warnings becoming ever more and more gentle," be helped to observe and correct what is faulty. Up to this point, "well-earned approbation, quietly but abundantly given out of a full heart, must be the spring upon which the force of an abundant, convincing, carefully apportioned blame must work. But when once *self*-education has begun it must not be interfered with. When the time arrives that the pupil possesses both praise and blame within himself, and can guide and impel himself by their means,"[1] the work of discipline is done.

---

[1] *Science of Education*, p. 248.

CHAPTER V

THE RELATIONSHIP AND DEBT OF HERBART TO PESTALOZZI[1]

THE history of human progress supplies us with the cheering fact that truth is indestructible. When an idea has a truth as its essence, the imperfections of its original embodiment are not only powerless to check its vitality and ultimate development, but are often a direct stimulus to both.

There is no more striking instance of this than is supplied by Herbart's relationship to Pestalozzi. At first sight it would appear that, from the great differences of birth, temperament, and education between these two men, their points of contact must be necessarily few and superficial. On the one hand is the intuitively taught man of genius, who, by his own confession, had not read a single book for thirty years, whose only literary attempt to systematize his mode of teaching, *Inquiry into the Course of Nature in the Development of the Human Race*, was a signal failure, and who repeatedly mourned over his "unpractical ideas," over "the contradiction between his will and his power," and his "inability to conduct the smallest village school"; on the other hand is the man of learning, whose rare original power of analytical and abstract thought had been developed to perfection by all that was most favourable in his home, in the school, and the university, and who was beginning to generalize his first successful experiences as a teacher into the principles of a new system of education. Such were Pestalozzi and Herbart, the former fifty-three, the latter twenty-three, years of age, when their first meeting took place at Burgdorf, a town not far from Berne, where Pestalozzi, fresh from "one of the most

---

[1] This chapter mainly appeared as an article in the *Journal of Education* for May, 1892, and is here reprinted with the kind permission of the Editor.

memorable events in the history of education "—*i.e.*, his five months' experiment at Stanz—was teaching the lowest class in the Citizens' School. Two years later Herbart described that meeting with generous enthusiasm; he recognized the success of Pestalozzi's teaching, and discerned in it that which we have seen was to Herbart himself the great aim of instruction, *i.e.* its *educative* value, as proved by "the vigorous stability of mind" the children gained from it. "I saw him," wrote Herbart, "in his schoolroom. A dozen children were assembled at an unusual hour in the evening." (Pestalozzi had summoned them for Herbart's inspection.) "I feared I should find them ill-tempered, should see the experiment I had come to witness fail; but they came without a sign of rebellion, and their state was one of lively activity till the end. I heard the noise of the whole school speaking together—no, not a noise, but a harmony of words, extremely distinct, powerful as a choir keeping time like one, and withal so closely and distinctly connected with what had just been taught, that I felt some difficulty in restraining myself from passing from my *rôle* of spectator into that of a learning child. I watched to discover possibly a silent or carelessly speaking child, but I found none. The intonation of these children pleased my ear, although their teacher had the most unintelligible voice imaginable, and their speech could not have been taught them by their Swiss parents. But the explanation was not far to seek. The rhythmic speech, pronounced simultaneously, produced distinct articulation, the syllables could not be slurred over, each letter had its time, and thus the child, speaking steadily aloud with his natural strength of voice, found utterance for himself. Nor was the general and sustained attention a riddle to me. The mouth and hands of each child were occupied together; inactivity and silence were imposed on none. Thus the need for distraction was done away with, and natural liveliness required no outlet, this way of learning together needing none. I was delighted with the ingenious use of the transparent horn tablet with incised letters, on which the children's hands were steadily engaged, while they were learning by heart. A silent but dexterous master corrected their pencilled letters, and encouraged them to do better. Even now, when I draw diagrams for mathematical demonstrations on the blackboard, I reprove my hand for its inability to produce such firm straight lines, such perfect perpendiculars and accurate circles, as did these six-year-old children; and I value far beyond this mere manual dexterity, the vigorous stability of mind which the children gain thus happily by keeping steadily to the idea of roundness, till the eager, purposing eye and the obedient hand slowly but surely complete the circle with a faultless curve."

Herbart saw that once more in the world's history the truth had entered in at lowly doors. Perceiving the value of the principle of observation (*Anschauung*), "that grand idea," as he calls it, "of its discoverer, the noble Pestalozzi," he afterwards made it the basis of one of his most important works (*Über Pestalozzi's Idee einer A B C der Anschauung*); through that work, the principle became one source of his great success as a mathematical teacher. "Pestalozzi," he writes, "has only worked out the application of the principle within the narrow sphere of elementary instruction. It belongs in truth to education as a whole, though it needs for that a further development."

To such a work Pestalozzi was quite unequal. We are told he was ignorant of drawing, and scorned grammatical learning. He was conversant with ordinary operations in arithmetic, but would have had difficulty in getting through a long sum in multiplication or division, and he probably had never tried to work out a problem in geometry.[1] This want of ordered knowledge and the circumstances of his environment combined to render him utterly incapable of such a task. His experiences and intuitions, which initiated a revolution in education, could accomplish wonderful things in the children immediately in contact with him, but his untrained mind could not work up these materials into a system.

In applying the principle of observation—*Anschauung*—to mathematics, Pestalozzi's choice of the square as the type

---

[1] *Life of Pestalozzi*, by Roger de Guimps.

figure, and Herbart's strictly reasoned rejection of the same and choice of the triangle in its place, illustrate at the very beginning of their respective works, the different manner in which the uneducated and educated man made use of the idea. Again, Pestalozzi attempted to give in his *ABC* the elements of arithmetic as well as of form, while Herbart only treated arithmetic incidentally, and then for advanced pupils alone. The measurement of *surface*, too, to which Pestalozzi attaches so much importance, occupies with Herbart a subordinate place. In its stead Herbart goes far deeper into mathematics, and really obtains by analysis phenomenal forms in space for the elements of his observation instruction. With his extended knowledge of psychology and mathematics, he did a work which Pestalozzi, theoretically ignorant of both, could not have attempted; the principle of *Anschauung*, which the Swiss philanthropist had divined rather than discovered, provides in the German philosopher's application of it what may truly be called a prologue to mathematics.

But Herbart always acknowledged that to Pestalozzi he was *directly* indebted for the idea which forms the basis of the work. Further, he saw that there were essential elements of similarity between his own aim and that of this teacher of the poor. Both knew the supreme importance, and therefore tried to find a true sequence of studies which should correspond to the advancing stages and parallel needs of the child's development. "To discover this sequence," writes Herbart, "is Pestalozzi's chief effort and likewise my own great ideal." And the fundamental belief which inspired the activity of both was one and the same. It was, that an education which gives the individual power to develop every faculty, intellectual and emotional, in the service of morality, is the one constant force which can elevate humanity. Hence, recognizing Pestalozzi as a fellow-labourer in a great and common cause, Herbart tried to make his work known and valued amongst a class to which Pestalozzi himself had no access.

Herbart's treatise on Pestalozzi's then recently published work, *Wie Gertrud ihre Kinder lehrt*, from which the description of his first meeting with Pestalozzi is taken, was, in his own words, "written to help the readers of Pestalozzi's book to form a correct estimate of it." The treatise was addressed to the wives of three of Herbart's friends—viz., to "three mothers" in Bremen—and through them to all mothers of the upper classes. Its object was to show that, Pestalozzi's principle being of universal application, it ought not to be confined to the children of the poor, but should be known and intelligently used by mothers of every class.

Pestalozzi, says Herbart to them, speaks of beggars' children. The ideal for their culture is supplied, he says, by agriculture, industry, trade, and these he will use instead of the usual wretched subjects of school instruction. His material must be a lever so stout that it will not break in clumsy hands. Perhaps you can hardly conceive *his* method can be of use to *you*. Let us see The most pressing needs are likewise the most universal. He who tries to provide what is most necessary for all, has something to say to us also.

What then is the most general, the most efficient, and therefore the primary element in all instruction? Nature and human beings surround the child. The most important thing to secure is, that the daily experience they offer to the child, the boy, the youth, the man, shall always find open doors and beaten paths to head and heart, that it may stimulate tongue and hand to answer to each moment's need. How is this to be effected? It is true, nature and human beings seek of themselves to find an entrance to the child through eye and ear; but they often block that entrance by the very multiplicity, brightness, and variety of their objects. People speak too quickly; nature shows too many forms in one field, too many colours in one flower. All this confusion does in a manner penetrate the child, because he is impelled by the liveliest necessity, and he learns to speak, to see, to touch. But do you think, when he can express to some extent his physical wants, he can *really* see, speak, and understand? By no means. If he looks only so superficially at things as is necessary to distinguish them from each other, is not the whole wealth of form with which nature surrounds him lost to him? Do you think your children will care to study the outline, the size, of countries on the map, or will your boys learn with interest natural history, technology, mechanics, geometry, physics, or be well prepared for their handiwork, if they cease to cultivate the eye, as soon as it has learned to serve their primary needs? It is just the same with speech. While then the need, the impulse, is in the child to articulate, to grasp the forms of things, at the period when he inquires the names of objects, and daily finds new ones which charm him into looking at them narrowly and from every side, *then* is the time, before this natural progress is at an end, when you must come to his help, and open out his sense for form and speech, that he may be able truly to see nature and receive thoughts. It is the eye which must first perceive objects before they can be named and talked about. Therefore practice in observation (*Anschauung*) is that primary, most effectual, most general principle of which we have been in search. Many have recommended its exercise, but Pestalozzi, so far as I know, was the first to insist that it, and it only, should occupy, as it ought, the first and foremost place.

But not only did Herbart point out the intellectual importance of Pestalozzi's principle: he recognized and appreciated the noble simplicity of the man, and his boundless devotion to his self-chosen cause. He saw that Pestalozzi, possessed with a sense of the misery and degradation of the poor, for whose relief his life was spent in unappreciated toil, had neither thought nor hope beyond their rescue, and these very limitations became in his kindly sight, a new reason for honouring and understanding the truth of his efforts and his purpose.

"The salvation of the people, of the common rough folk," writes Herbart to these more favoured mothers, " is Pestalozzi's aim. For those who are the least cared for, *he* cares. In huts, not in your houses, he seeks his crown of reward. This kindly, lovable man of sixty years, who greets everything human with such gentleness, whose first word to the stranger seems to say, 'Here he who deserves it will find a heart'—you mothers of the upper classes will not reproach him because, full of pain at the signs of the times and the misery of his fellow-men, he cuts his way down, as one impelled by the enthusiasm of youth, to the lowest class of all, in order to teach its little children their letters, and pours out vehement words there, when a cool, accurate description of his method would be to *us* more welcome and instructive. To give *you* useful advice is only a thing by the way to *him*. This will not prejudice you against him. You will surely be interested as easily, as happily, in all which the activity of such a man works upon and seeks to penetrate. And you must preserve this feeling while you study his work, or you will neither be able to recognize the purpose of his effort, nor rightly determine the use you can make of it."

No less clearly did Herbart perceive what he would have termed the educative value, the moral influence, of Pestalozzi's instruction. By means of the senses it develops and perfects in useful exercise, *that* interest in things external to the child is generated, which Herbart taught was the true preventive of early selfishness and a preparation of the mind for the teacher's after-work. Such an interest fosters in the child a natural forgetfulness of self, and in so doing preserves "the childlike mind, the unconscious look straight into the world, which seeks nothing, and for that very reason sees what is to be seen."[1] The relation between his own and Pestalozzi's thought is very apparent in the following estimate by him of the ethical value of Pestalozzi's teaching :—

"To promote the intercourse of a human being with his fellow-men is Pestalozzi's aim. Does he in this do anything for morality? In silence perhaps just that is accomplished, which the moral lessons and pathetic stories written for children assume to be already existent. The *ground* is made ready for them where they can take root. The child, whose eye and ear are open to nature and his fellow-creatures, is diverted from his own manifold impressions, from his own pleasure or discomfort. Egoism is undermined in him, who attends not to himself, but to others and to the relationships of objects. Such an one is prepared to look at himself as one among many, and

---

[1] *Science of Education*, p. 246.

hence will speedily find the place for which he is fitted. When this general outlook at the relationships of men has become the ruling direction of the mind, it leads spontaneously and infallibly to the love of order therein, and to the preservation of that order by law and custom. *Afterwards*, when the roots of moral feeling have grown, is the time to direct the child's attention to himself, that he may win self-control, analyze and purify his opinions with watchful criticism, and devote his powers to recognized ends."

CHAPTER VI

CONCLUSION.—SOME ASPECTS OF HERBART'S WORK AND CHARACTER

'EDUCATION is work; and like every work, it has on the one hand its aim, on the other its means and obstacles. The aim of education raises us into the realm of the ideal; its means and obstacles take us back into the land of the actual—yes, of the veriest commonplace. In all great men who have thought and written about education, from Plato to Fichte, there is the striving towards an ideal; how, indeed, could it be otherwise? Without an exalted aim, how could the spirit of the man bear to bend down to that of the child; without the hope with which we look at the young, how could we conquer the coldness of the thought that, in spite of all effort, the world will remain as it is?"[1]

The teacher's work, the path of its progress, the difficulties and discouragements it meets with on its arduous way, the promise and hope of its great reward—Herbart's knowledge of these was gathered up by the combined force of enthusiasm and a rare ability, through the study and practical experiences of a lifetime. Not without interest, therefore, can it be to indicate in conclusion, what are the aspects of his work, and what the features of his character as revealed therein, which appeal to the intelligence and reverence of the true teacher.

First, education was accepted and carried on by him, not merely as a duty or means of livelihood. Including these, it went far beyond them; it was to him a chosen, a loved, a sacred task. "The offer of the whole treasure of accumulated research in a concentrated form to the youthful generation,"

---

[1] *Aphorismen zur Pädagogik*, Herbart.

says he, "is the highest service which man at any period of his existence can render to his successors."

"The happiness of the teacher! He who seeks a happiness outside the inner sanctuary of his own circle of ideas, which shall carry with it a reasonable delight, and not spring from chance, can gain it only from a work whose aim is the revelation of ideas to an existing intelligence." Few have maintained so consistently and so highly as he, in deed and word, the beauty and dignity of the teacher's calling.

Again, education was not to him, as to every other great modern thinker who has approached it, an outlying field wherein his mental powers were only active at intervals. It was the point towards which his great store of metaphysical, psychological, and ethical knowledge converged; it was the very focus of his activity. Half his adult life was chiefly spent in laying the scientific foundations of education, an important part of the other half in constructing it on that basis, in the light of his philosophy, into a scientific system. "For twenty years," he writes, "I have called to my aid metaphysics and mathematics, besides self-observation, experience, and experiments, in order only to lay the foundation of true psychologic knowledge. And the impulse to these not easy investigations was, and is, my conviction that a great portion of the enormous defects in our educational knowledge arises from the want of psychology."

The preceding passage supplies one reason of Herbart's great success as a teacher—*i.e.*, his knowledge of both the principles and practice of education. Science and empiricism, the theory and the art of teaching, both are indispensable to him who would surely and successfully guide the mind of another. Herbart's attempt to teach his students the art of education has been elsewhere described, and need only be alluded to here as the result of his conviction, that "education cannot be merely taught, but must be also demonstrated and practised." But his insistence that a knowledge of the art of education could never dispense with or supply any deficiency in the knowledge of its theory, is yet more emphatic, for he held it to be of primary importance. To those who would base education on experience *alone*, he points out, the nature of educational experience is such that it demands a great part of a lifetime for its growth and ingathering. "No one," he says, "has a right to speak of experience until the experiment is completed, until, above all things, the residuum has been accurately weighed and tested. In the case of educational experiments, this residuum is represented by the faults of the pupil when he has attained to manhood. Thus the time required for one such experiment is at least half a human life." Experience must determine how and to what extent the principles of theoretic pedagogy can be utilized without injuring the personality of the pupil. "The true educator makes it a point of honour that the clear impression of the person, the family, the birth, and the nationality, may be seen undefaced in the man submitted to his will," and the knowledge of the pupil's individuality which can alone make this possible nothing but experience can supply. But, argues Herbart, only those who have mastered the science of education, can thoroughly understand how to collect, interpret, and use experience. "Nowhere," says he, "is philosophic breadth of vision so necessary as in teaching, where daily practice and individual experience, expressed in such a variety of ways, so greatly narrow its range of view. Thus a preparation for the art by the science is necessary, a preparation of the understanding and the heart before entering on the work, in virtue of which experience, which we can alone get by actual doing of the work, will yield to us its lessons. In practice only is the art learned, and tact, readiness, versatility, and skill acquired; but art teaches by practice him alone who has previously learned his science in thought, made it his own, formed himself by it, and predetermined the future impressions which experience ought to make on him."[1]

---

[1] Herbart's insistence on the necessity of a scientific training for teachers may be considered with profit at the present moment, when the reproach that no training college for secondary schoolmasters exists in England is about to be taken away by the opening of one in connection with the College of Preceptors. It is to be hoped, in the interests of English education, that it will not share the fate of its predecessor through the unwillingness of male teachers to recognize

In sharp contrast with Locke, who calls "instruction the least part of education," Herbart, on the basis of his psychology, proves it to be the most important part. Locke, the utilitarian, with regard to intellectual education, separates distinctly from it the ethical side of culture, and places, like Herbart, the perfection of the latter—*i.e.*, virtue, morality—as the great aim of education. Relegating intellectual culture to a secondary place and setting before it the lower aim of utility, Locke consistently calls instruction the least part of education. In doing so, he takes but little account of that relation between moral and intellectual enlightenment, which was to Herbart an indissoluble and intimate interaction, formed and maintained by instruction through its cultivation in the circle of thought, of both will and insight, the moral and intellectual in man. As the factor which determines, through the wealth and the nature of the presentations it supplies, the extent and perfection of this interaction, Herbart held instruction to be the most important part of education. Roughly speaking, the teacher is he who supplies the presentations, the material for the circle of thought, the pupil he who receives it, but there is a qualifying element in Herbart's conception of this relationship between teacher and pupil, which cannot be too clearly kept in view by those who would grasp its full significance. This element is *the individuality of the pupil*. The teacher's vast and noble work is to penetrate the innermost core of the mind germ entrusted to his keeping, that he may, as it were, inoculate it with thoughts, feelings, and desires it could never otherwise have obtained, which when absorbed into itself will continuously help to guide and determine its after-growth. But in doing so he must respect the personality itself, and keep its better part intact. "The teacher," says Herbart, "ought to make it a point of honour to leave the individuality as untouched as possible; he ought to leave to it the only glory of which it is capable,

---

the necessity of training, and their disinclination to accept those opportunities for it, of which English women have made such extensive and successful use.

namely, to be sharply defined and recognized even to conspicuousness, that the specimen of the race may not appear insignificant by the side of the race itself and vanish as indifferent."

Closely bound up with the recognition of the supreme claim of the individuality to its own self-development, is Herbart's conception of the ideal which the teacher must ever keep in sight from the beginning of his work to its end, viz., to develop in the pupil, *through his own active self-doing*, the knowledge and the use of ordered liberty. " A making," he says, " which the pupil himself discovers when choosing the good and rejecting the bad—this or nothing is formation of character." Only so far as the teacher "places the power already existent, and in its nature trustworthy, under such conditions that it must infallibly and surely accomplish this rise to self-conscious personality," does he perform his work aright. The greater the ability of the teacher who neglects to appeal to and strengthen this power by constant use, the greater, according to Herbart, will be the extent of his failure. Such a teacher was Fenelon. "Through his ability, he was too successful in his educational apostleship. Under his hand, the ablest, says St. Simon, that ever was, the Duke de Bourgogne, became a pale copy of his master. Fenelon had monopolized and absorbed the will of his pupil."[1] Far other was that ideal which Herbart kept before himself throughout his life, and expressed, when a young teacher, to his first pupils in these words: "No human power ought to be crippled; all ought to advance to perfection under the protection and gentle rule of the moral law." The pupil of Fenelon was as the image and superscription of his master, accurate and clear, cast by him in his own mould. The pupil of Herbart was as a ship able to adapt itself to every change of wind and wave, steered towards its goal at first by the teacher's hand, and afterwards by the cultivated and self-won power of the pupil himself.

So far as to the aspects of Herbart's work. Certain features of his character are specially noticeable as revealed therein.

---

[1] *History of Pedagogy*, by Gabriel Compayre.

First, that which he set up as the immediate aim of intruction—many-sided interest—he realized and perfected in himself. The reader will find abundant evidence in his works of his interest arising from knowledge, empirical, speculative, and æsthetic; his interest arising from sympathy, whether with individuals, with society, or with religion, was a hardly less prominent characteristic. His relationship to Pestalozzi, described in the preceding chapter, is one instance among many wherein were combined elements of both interests which passed into fruitful thought and act. That he could recognize and appropriate the idea of a teacher on such a different plane of culture from himself as Pestalozzi, and afterwards apply it in a direction and to a degree never dreamed of by its originator, is an instance of his intellectual many-sidedness. That he could see with discriminating insight and generous enthusiasm, and attempt to make others see, this loftiness of Pestalozzi's ideal and the ethical value of his teaching, is a no less striking instance of his large-hearted and many-sided sympathy.

But by far the most prominent feature of his character was his reverence, his passion for truth.

"To penetrate the sacred depths of truth,
To strive in joyful hope for human weal,
Was his life's aim."

These words, engraven on his tombstone, contain the history of his life, and they are the central thought of all that has been worthily written in his memory. This reverence for truth was fed by all the forces of his intellectual and moral nature. His absorbing desire for it, combined with his firm belief that an overruling Providence had given the power of discovering it to humanity, produced in him that steadfast will which never swerved from its pursuit in an age whose spi it was opposed to the course of his thought. That philosophic inquiry must be absolutely independent of all which is external to the necessary course of thought, was to him an inevitable presumption of scientific investigation. Hence he could not understand the efforts contemporary philosophers made to defend their position against attacks and criticisms based on subjective feeling or on external authority. Still less could he understand those newer speculative systems which made what they called speculative theology their main centre. For the same penetration which showed him so clearly the necessary conditions of investigation and verification, showed him also, that there were regions where such conditions cannot obtain, and hence where no exact knowledge is possible. His efforts, so visible in his writings, to free philosophy from the influence of theology were caused by his belief that, while theology could at best do little to forward philosophy, its general tendency was to hinder and even oppose the course of philosophical research. But they were also caused by his abiding conviction, that the nature of the *subject* of religious belief made it an impossible *object* for speculative inquiry. Beyond the region of the known and the knowable still unknown, he felt the unknowable, an infinite the human mind could not measure, but whose outskirts it could only touch by subjective effort, the results of which effort, being incapable of objective proof, could never claim universal validity. Allowing this conviction its full force in determining the unpassable boundaries of his philosophic inquiries, he separated himself from one important side of the thought of his time. But he preserved what was to him the life-blood of his mind, its integrity, and in so doing satisfied then, as ever, that passion for truth to which he dedicated his whole and willing service.

But it was in that ultimate Reality which can neither be apprehended by the senses nor reached alone by the reason that Herbart sought and found the full answer to his hope and love. In his own words, " his mind kept Sabbath in religion." He " turned to it " not as knowledge, but as hope, founded on what he held to be the evidence of design in nature, " for rest from all thoughts, desires, and cares."[1] And this he did, not with the exclusiveness of the philosopher, but with the ever-present sense that religion was a universal response in a variety of tongues to the common need of man. Memorable, when

---

[1] *Science of Education*, p. 175.

taken in this connection, are the words which, as the honoured successor of one of the greatest thinkers of modern times, he spoke in his memory, " Religion is older than any earthly wisdom; the need of it is born with every child of man, and the invisible Lord receives with equal goodness all hearts which dedicate themselves to Him."[1]

In his *Rede über Fichte's Ansicht der Weltgeschichte* there is on the one hand this fervent belief in a Divine order of the world, on the other the veracity of thought which perceived that the belief, which was a great reality to him, could be exhibited to other minds as hypothesis only. The cause which Herbart believed to underlie phenomena could not be observed by human faculties; hence he knew the assumption of such a cause could only commend itself for acceptance to other minds, to the extent to which it succeeded in explaining diverse facts, or in reducing partial laws to harmony. Fichte had called the century in which they lived " the age of completed sinfulness." This age, said Fichte, in consolation and explanation, is a necessary transition from the period when men were guided by a reason acting as instinct, to another when they will have learned, as the lesson of their long errors and wanderings, to answer of their own free will to the guidance of reason. To Herbart a theory which consciously sacrificed one generation of men to another, was a false explanation of the world, and as such he rejected it. His conviction was " that humanity is good in its essence, and that the true earthly preparation for a future higher state of existence is never wanting to any race or age." But he carefully points out to his hearers that the theory he offers as substitute contains no more *knowledge* than the one rejected. That which had become to him a truth of belief must be judged by others by its power to explain and reconcile phenomena. " The consolation for ' this age of sinfulness ' is to be found rather in the old idea that the earthly life is a school for the immortal soul, not for the race, but for every individual, of which no one is sacrificed for another, as in Fichte's theory of earlier generations

---

[1] *Rede gehalten an Geburtstage Kant's*, April 22nd, 1810.

sunk in sin, that later ones may attain to knowledge and art. Far otherwise run the lessons of history, and, as I am bound to add, the teaching of philosophy. History, never concealing, but plainly revealing, all the crooked ways along which mankind has passed, sometimes madly rushing, sometimes slowly creeping, says nothing of a world-plan, according to which all were compelled from the beginning to move straight forwards, or at least in one and the same devious line appointed by law. All the more clearly and emphatically, however, does history show us ever and always the same humanity, with the same needs, the like passions, only with variations explicable through different modes of life, knowledge, and purposed culture. A psychologic unity and obedience to law is herein apparent; it comes of itself freely to meet philosophy, which discovers as a necessity just the same obedience to law, with small and slow changes, due to the increase of ideas and insight, as well as to the growth and decay of error and passion. In the old and the uniform, in that which always repeats itself during immeasurable centuries with some progress, lies the nature of man, and therein must we seek for the gifts of God. According to the Divine order, man comes helpless into the world, but capable of cultivation by language, family, reciprocal needs, accumulated experience, discovered arts, existing science, the works of genius from all preceding ages, which, the longer their duration, must the more uniformly influence ages to come. Humanity becomes ever more matured, living on always under the same sun, on the same earth. The salutary powers by means of which it ripens are, although the least observed, ever the same and ever active. The changing fortunes of humanity are like the mountains on the earth's surface. They show as little regularity as those mountains, and vainly do we try to imagine it. But the sphere of the earth is as a whole well rounded, and human history, the longer its course, cannot fail to trace ever more clearly and distinctly that straight line which it must traverse according to psychologic laws, under conditions ordered in the beginning by God." [1]

---

[1] *Rede über Fichte's Ansicht der Weltgeschichte*, from Hartenstein's edition of *Herbart's Sämmtliche Werke*, vol. xii. p. 247.

Conclusion.—Some Aspects of Herbart's Work and Character

Herbart's theory of the order of the world contained in the preceding passage is compressed by him into his pregnant saying, "Humanity educates itself continuously by the circle of thought which it begets."[1] In the order of nature, as learned and interpreted by the developing faculties of man, he saw a divine provision for the education of the race; he saw, too, that the true teacher, as the interpreter of that order, moves forward as a co-worker with Providence under the divine sanction and aid. In this progress lay his hope for humanity, in its power to forward this progress, his faith in education.

---

[1] *Science of Education*, p. 93.

Cloth. 268 pages. $1.00.

THE
Science of Education;
Its General Principles Deduced from Its Aim,

AND

THE ÆSTHETIC REVELATION OF THE WORLD.

BY

JOHANN FRIEDRICH HERBART,
Professor of Philosophy at the University of Göttingen.

Translated from the German, with a Biographical Introduction by
HENRY M. and EMMIE FELKIN,

AND A

Preface by OSCAR BROWNING, M.A., Fellow of King's College, Cambridge.

OPINIONS OF THE PRESS.

"Mr. and Mrs. Felkin have earned the gratitude of the educationists of this country in presenting this admirable translation of some of the greatest of the works on a great subject."—*The Scotsman.*

"Exceptionally well executed. Herbart was without doubt the most important of the post-Kantian philosophers of Germany, with the exception of Hegel, and although more than half a century has elapsed since he left us, his ideas, corresponding in some degree with those of Mill and Bain and Spencer among ourselves, have been of the nature of those that have most powerfully influenced our age. We are unquestionably the better, having a book like this thrust upon our attention—a book written by one of the few really great theorists on education. The volume is a valuable addition to our gradually growing educational library."—*The Glasgow Herald.*

"The work is of enormous value. It will supply a foundation on which a real science of education may be built. The book has

been admirably translated by Mr. Henry Felkin and Mrs. Felkin."
—*Westminster Review.*

"To adopt the words of Emerson, many people, indeed all but a handful, would 'as soon think of swimming across Charles River to go to Boston,' as of reading Herbart in the original, now that there is so careful and exact an English translation as this of Mr. and Mrs. Felkin. This is a book of thoughts, of Herbart's thoughts; and the nearness with which a reader is brought to him, even the word-for-word nearness, is often helpful, not to say essential. It is not superfluous to repeat one's word of thanks to the translators for what must have been anxious and laborious work."—*The Academy.*

"Full of facts and suggestions that will prove most valuable to all responsible, whether as guardians or schoolmasters, for the educational training of others. The whole work should be carefully studied by the historian of education as well as by the practical teacher; to both it will be most serviceable."—*The Athenæum.*

"In brief, this is a book for every teacher to read in with profit, but it is a book that few teachers will care even to read through. Sit down to it and you are dismayed; glance through it and you are delighted with the wisdom it contains."—*Educational Review.*

"Now that this Science of Education is restored to light it should be in every library of educational works for reference and comparison. We are therefore doubly grateful to Mr. and Mrs. Felkin for their public-spirited labours, and congratulate them on their result."— *Educational Times.*

"Every page of his work breathes the true spirit of teaching. A work of this character is invaluable in the hands of tutors and masters of method. It leads one into the true science of teaching, and must exert a strong influence towards the destruction of false and shallow conceptions of the pedagogic art."—*Schoolmaster.*

"The volume is full of philosophy of the deepest interest, and contains much of Herbart's best thought. Herbart's system may not be possible of adoption in its entirety under any circumstances, but those afforded by tuition, under which conditions he, of course, practised it, but many of the broad principles would greatly benefit the pupils in our large schools."—*Nottingham Guardian.*

D. C. HEATH & CO., Publishers, Boston, New York, Chicago.

www.ingramcontent.com/pod-product-compliance
Lightning Source LLC
Chambersburg PA
CBHW020907230426
43666CB00008B/1348